You're Worth It !

INVESTMENT STRATEGIES FOR WOMEN

A NOVEL APPROACH

Gail Kennedy

Canadian Cataloguing in Publication Data

Kennedy, Gail
 You're Worth It! : investment strategies for women : a novel approach

ISBN 0-9698974-0-5

1. Investments. 2. Women--Finance, Personal. I. Title
HG 4528.K45 1994   332.6'78   C94-900909-1

Published and Distributed by:
 Raintree Communications Inc.
First published November, 1994

Printed in Canada by:
 Milgrom & Associates Inc.
 Integrated Communications:
 755 The Queensway East, Suite 105
 Mississauga, Ontario L4Y 4C5
 1-905-897-7555

ISBN 0-969-89740-5

*Dedicated to the loving memory
of my mother Ferne E. Kennedy*

CONTENTS

Introduction

You're Worth It! has been written for women who have the desire to learn the ins and outs of the financial markets and employ their capital smartly. Investing in stocks, bonds and mutual funds is the best way to increase your hard-earned money over a long period of time. However, selecting investments without understanding what effect the market and economic conditions can have on your portfolio is very dangerous.

For years, I have been concerned that women are not taking advantage of the opportunities available to help build their financial net worth and ultimately secure their futures. I also know that some women who are currently investing may not fully understand the investments that they are buying. Millions of women have neglected the financial part of their education, but the world is changing and it is now more important than ever for women to become involved in and knowledgeable about their financial affairs. Gone are the days when men were solely responsible for women's financial well-being.

Back in the '70s, when I was managing a trust company office, a woman asked the receptionist if she could speak to the manager. The receptionist offered her a seat and said, "I'll get her."

"Her!" the woman said, as she stood to leave, "I don't want to talk to a woman."

It took a long time to convince this woman that I was competent to deal with her situation. She only agreed to stay when I promised to provide a male colleague if she asked me a question that I was unable to answer.

The securities industry is still male dominated, as is the senior management of most banks and trust companies, but the attitudes of women have changed over the years. Many of us shy away from male financial advisors. We are not confident that we'll ask the proper questions and fear that we may be patronized or criticised as we attempt to put our financial houses in order.

I have worked in the financial industry for over 25 years and know that it'll be decades before this situation changes. Women can't wait. I have been financially dependent, financially co-dependent, and finally financially independent, and

I know that the key to financial success is knowledge. Educated women - I'm not talking about women who have successfully obtained an MBA, but those who have taken the time to learn and understand the market and participate in it - are financially rewarded.

Begin your education with *You're Worth It!*

Most books on this subject are presented in a technical format which may be boring and difficult to understand, let alone finish. *You're Worth It!* is written in a narrative style, with fictional characters, and carries you through from beginning to end in an informal, relaxed manner. You will meet a group of women, neighbours who after discovering their financial exposure, learn together over the cold winter months. They emerge in the spring confident and more knowledgeable about the financial world and making clear investment decisions. If you follow the steps that the women in the book do, you, too, will be on your way to financial independence. I encourage you to gather information as they do. Use the book as a guide. Phone numbers and addresses of many of the institutions you'll want to contact are listed at the end of it.

When you've finished reading *You're Worth It!* the financial world will make more sense to you. You will understand the fundamentals of the market and the conditions that affect it. You will be able to make investment decisions relatively easily. You will understand the importance of time and timing and be able to avoid making disastrous errors. You will see the value of diversification, which will help eliminate any fear you may have of investing.

But most of all, you will be confident enough to pick up the phone and begin working with a financial advisor. You will find that once you have a fundamental understanding of the investment world, your comfort level will increase and your fear of investing will disappear.

I give you my 25 years (plus) of experience and knowledge. Use it well to secure your future.

Remember, *you're worth it!*
Gail

Acknowledgements

I didn't realize, when I began, what an enormous task I had undertaken. I foolishly thought that I'd be able to whip-off the first draft of this book within a few weeks. Well, it has taken me 14 months, 12 days, six hours and 37 minutes to reach this final stage and I wouldn't be here yet, if it weren't for a number of friends, colleagues and interested people who believed that this subject and my approach to it were important.

For the many encouraging words throughout the process, special thanks to my closest friend and former colleague, Theresa Currie, Senior Vice President, Multiple Retirement Services, Inc., who , when I became discouraged, was always there, pulling me back on track.

There are some people in this world who enter your life late but have such a tremendous impact that words of thanks are just not enough. Irwin Milgrom is this person in my life. His genuine concern and encouragement is one of the reasons *You're Worth It!* became a reality. Thank you Irwin and thanks also to your special wife Stella, whose continual enthusiasm and guidance helped keep me going.

George Hartman, author of *Risk Is A Four Letter Word*, is responsible for the book being in its current format. "Write a book that the people will enjoy reading while learning," he advised. Thank you, George - I wrote with your valuable comments in mind.

In addition to these key people, technical expertise came from Ray Chang, President of Canadian International Group, who read and read and read from the beginning to the completion and provided the reality checks so desperately needed when a non-technical mind writes. There are many others who have supported this endeavour. However, I'd like to especially thank Marilyn Buttery of The Investment Centre, Marilyn Thomas of Vancouver, Gill Chandler of RBC Dominion Securities and Colin Haddock, Chartered Accountant. Your comments and insight have been most helpful.

Gail Wright, Regional Vice-President of C.I. Mutual Funds, supported this endeavour from the beginning. Thank you Gail for being there.

If this book had to be typed on a manual typewriter it would have consisted of 25 pages at best. But I am fortunate to have as a good friend the most competent computer person in North America. Tony Issa was there for me day and night. Thank you, Tony, for your patience and continuous assistance.

You're Worth It! has been circulating in my mind for at least 20 years and thanks to the expertise of my editor, Linda Kenyon, it is finally on paper. Linda possessed the talent to become my beacon in a sea of words and had the patience to guide me through to the end. I am thoroughly convinced that had Linda sailed with and guided Columbus, he would have reached America months earlier. Thank you Linda.

And last but not least, Gerry, my better half, my in-house critic. I couldn't or wouldn't have done it without you.

Thank you.
Gail

Chapter One
September

Cathy lay under a tree, out of the sun, with a tattered old straw hat completely covering her face. She had had several potentially cancerous spots removed the year before, and was terrified of the sun. But the rest of us couldn't have cared less. We kept shedding more and more of our clothes to expose as much skin as possible. If anyone had ventured into the back yard, they would have encountered quite a sight: six women, most of us out of shape, yet there we were, reclining like sun goddesses.

We were enjoying one of our once-a-month Sunday afternoon get-togethers. They have become a reprieve for us, a chance to catch our breath, a time to escape from the day-to-day stress of life.

Most of us are over 40, although no one ever mentions age. Not that it bothers me. The older I get the smarter I become. That, at least, is my perception.

I am 48 and proud of it. I am successful, single, and going grey. My mother constantly nags, "Why don't you dye your hair, it ages you, cut it short, women over 30 shouldn't wear their hair longer than shoulder length." But I like my grey hair long, because I can wrap an elastic band around it and create a ponytail. Very sensible, I think.

She means well, she just can't figure me out.

I lead a casual life. I work such long hours, there isn't time for me to fuss. All my time and energy is focused on my career and it has paid off because I've become one of the top real estate brokers in our area. I love the business - it provides me with an excellent income and the freedom to do what I want, when I want.

Some of that freedom comes from owning my own firm. Currently I have seven other people on the sales staff. We specialize in the high end of the market, homes that have very high price tags. It takes us longer to make a sale, but when we do, we earn a large commission.

I went to work right after high school as a receptionist in a real estate office near my parents' home, where I lived without paying rent for the first five years out in the working world. This situation really suited me, but I realized that my welcome was over when my dad lent me $5,000 as a down payment on a small house. I suspect the loan was the price of their freedom. I'm sure they thought that if they didn't help, I would never move out.

I bought a small bungalow which I then fixed up and sold. I made a hefty profit and bought another. I've owned six homes in ten years, making substantial profits each time I sold. Twelve years ago, I bought the home I live in now.

By then, I had become quite successful in my niche market and finally settled down and stopped moving. My home is free and clear, thanks to the profits made on my previous real estate transactions, and my income averages between $75,000 and $150,000 each year.

I am quite content.

But I haven't always been. Over the years I've made a name for myself as an outspoken advocate of women's rights. I think it started back in grade school.

I remember my dad instructing the teachers to force me to write with my right hand. I was a natural lefty, but for the first year of school, under the constant eye of the teacher, I sat on my left hand as I struggled to learn how to write with my right. Dad's thinking was that, being a girl, I was limited in my career choices. A teacher, nurse or secretary were my options. If I became a secretary (this is before the invention of the ballpoint pen), I would smear my writing with my back-handed approach. I don't remember being angry, but I am sure that I must have been humiliated.

I realized early in life that different things were expected from girls than from boys. My friend Mary was the toughest tomboy that ever lived. She beat up so many boys, they would cross the street to avoid her. When we were very young, her aunt gave her a huge doll for her birthday. The thing had to be three feet tall. We gathered up all the rope we could find, strung this little princess from a tree and beat it to shreds with our baseball bats. I remember her aunt crying and her mother chasing us. Mary's father stood in the doorway and laughed. Maybe he knew something we didn't. Today, Mary has been married for 28 years and has two children of her own. I suspect, if there is any justice in this world, that her daughter gives her the same grief that we caused our parents. Through my teens and in my early adult years, my friends and I were considered rebels. We marched, yelled and wreaked all kinds of havoc on any group that we disagreed with as far as women's rights were concerned. We felt unless we were disruptive, we would not be heard.

I look back with pride over that period of time in my life, because I know we were very much responsible for some of the advancement women have made. But I don't have the energy for it anymore. Or maybe I have started to mellow.

I suppose, if I had married, I might have started to mellow sooner, but I didn't. They say that 10 percent of women today will not marry, so I guess I have become a statistic. It's not that I haven't had the opportunity - I have, but I haven't met a man that didn't require a major make-over in order to provide me with the freedom to pursue life as I think it should be lived. The older I get, the tougher my standards grow. In fact, there probably isn't a man today that could meet them or at least cause me to adjust my lifestyle to let him in.

Lonely?

Sometimes. Years ago when I attended the weddings of my friends, my single life really hit home, and then, when their children were born, I would go into a depression. It wouldn't last long however - my work needed as much care, hard work and long hours as raising any child. And I'm certainly less lonely now that the women in the neighbourhood have been getting together once a month.

Ruth and I are closer than the rest of the group. We have lived next door to each other for 12 years and she is my best friend, which is amazing because we are so different. I love Ruth, but she certainly has strong old-fashioned views. She always disagrees with me. "Let things be," she says. "You can't change the world. A woman's place is in the home, taking care of the children and taking care of your husband's needs."

Ruth is the oldest of us all. I know that she is in her early 60s although she looks much younger. She keeps her hair coloured, but quite natural looking. She is always made up. Her eye-make-up, blush and hair are always perfect. I've never seen Ruth without lipstick - in fact, I accused her one time of having had a permanent lip colour treatment.

As I said, we are very different.

Ruth has never worked outside the home. Her husband is a successful marketing executive with a large international company. Bob is one of the nicest guys in the world. Ruth raised their children until they went off to university and has been the perfect hostess for all of Bob's clients, entertaining at least once every few weeks for 15 years.

Her house is immaculate and she always seems busy.

It was Ruth who introduced me to Cathy a few years ago. Cathy and I are approximately the same age and she is in her second marriage, to Cal. They have been married for 10 years and seemed relatively happy. Cathy is almost as much of a feminist as I am and it is she who supports my thoughts when I get on my soap box. She is a sixth grade teacher at the local elementary school.

It was the three of us who decided that an annual barbeque would bring the neighbourhood closer together. With its trimmed lawns and perfectly colour co-ordinated flower gardens, our neighbourhood is older and well established. It is a nice place to live.

We began organizing the barbeque in April and enlisted the help of Annette, who lives at the end of the street. Annie, as we call her, is the youngest of the group. She's probably in her early 30s, and is the only one with a small child, Brett, who is two years old. She works at a full-time job, and her husband Mark is in business for himself.

It is Annie who I have the most compassion for. Working, taking care of Brett. She must be so tired, yet I see little evidence of this. She is a buyer for a large international company which distributes educational products, mainly to schools.

I see her in the morning when I step out to retrieve my newspaper at 7:30. She has a huge sack of Brett's things under one arm, Brett in tow in one hand, her briefcase in the other and is heading for her car to take him to the baby-sitter. Brett carries a huge teddy bear which he manages to drop several times before they successfully reach the car door. She is always smiling and patient with him. She is so full of energy. I guess that's why it is smart to have babies when you are young. I get exhausted just watching her go through this routine every morning, knowing also that it has probably taken two hours to get to this stage. She works a full eight hour day and Mark picks the baby up at the end of the day. This routine is repeated five days a week, as regular as clockwork.

Oh well! To each their own, I think as I retreat to my kitchen for coffee which I drink while browsing through the real estate section of the paper. This is the start of my daily routine.

I can't help but take comfort knowing that my life choice has been right for me, but then I've not been doing my part in creating future home buyers and I surely will be alone during the latter part of my life. Maybe I should become a surrogate grandmother for Brett.

Grandmother! Whatever am I thinking. I must be going over the edge.

After the first barbecue in June, which was scheduled to end by 2:30 in the afternoon to allow the men time to watch the Blue Jays' game, the four organizers, Cathy, Annie, Ruth and I, began the clean up.

"What a mess!" Annie said. "Why is it that women are always expected to clean up?" she protested, as she carried a pile of soggy paper plates in one hand, walking bent over to ensure the grasp she had on Brett's hand didn't slip as she attempted to toss her pile of plates in the garbage. "Next year the barbecue will not be arranged around whatever sporting event happens to be on the TV. They think, as though it is their God given right, that as soon as dinner is over it is quite alright to disappear and leave the mess. Is it possible that they think one of us is going to wiggle our little nose and this disaster will disappear?"

Maybe she was more disturbed at having to watch Brett than at the mess we were left with. When she came back from putting him down for his nap, she was furious. Apparently, after she had put the little guy in bed and was returning to the back yard, she passed the men who were in a heated discussion over a bad play in the ball game. She said to Mark, "I've put the baby down for his nap. Will you listen for him, please?"

Mark said, as he sipped his beer, "Okay, I'll call you when he wakes up."

"Pardon! What did you say?" Annie stammered.

He repeated, "I'll call you when he wakes up."

"I don't think so - you take care of him for a while, this is my day off as well. I'll remind you that you golfed yesterday," she stated firmly. Annie stormed out the back door and began cleaning and muttering to herself. Before we could get her to sit down and talk, she had cleaned most of the yard.

"Calm down," Cathy comforted as she offered Annie a chair. "Sit down and relax and give us a chance to visit and get to know each other better."

And get to know each other we did.

After that day in June, we continued to get together once a month, always on a Sunday afternoon so that we wouldn't be missed, and we talked about everything under the sun. We discussed children, sex, jobs, bosses and co-workers, husbands, our pasts and our futures. We became quite close over the summer and began to rely on each other for support, information, sympathy, if needed, and just plain help.

I guess for some of us it was an escape. It certainly was for Annie, as Mark agreed to baby-sit once a month so Annie could join us. Needless to say, our first discussion centred around the inconsideration of men and their egos which, we concluded, none of us could understand. Men just don't think like women.

That first gathering formed the model for our future monthly meetings. They weren't meant to be gripe sessions, but it seemed that every once in a while, we ended up complaining about one thing or another. The meetings were by no means depressing, because each time we came away enlightened, as though the sharing of our thoughts and ideas had removed a burden or at least had lessened the load. We took comfort in knowing that we were not alone. Each one of us was struggling with our own problems.

In July, Cathy invited Elizabeth, who lived across the street, to join us. Liz, as she wanted to be called, was an absolute delight and she instantly fit in with our little group. She is somewhere in her mid 50s, a vibrant, well-spoken, striking woman.

She is divorced and retired. When we first met her, we all mulled this combination over in our minds. Most divorced women struggle all of their working lives just to make ends meet and some never reach the point of retirement, let alone doing so at such a young age. I know that I assumed that she must have received a large divorce settlement or was being supported by a wealthy ex-husband.

We spent the July session discussing her situation. Our hearts went out to her as she told us that she had been married to a lawyer and after 21 years of marriage, which she had thought were pretty good, he came home one day, packed his clothes, wished her well and left the number of a lawyer for her to contact about a divorce.

So much for the good marriage. No explanation, just good-bye. It devastated her. She told us how she cried and didn't sleep for weeks, until she became physically ill. Her family physician prescribed a sedative and over the next eight months she never left the house, lost 32 pounds and became addicted to the tranquillizer. During her months of obscurity, her husband liquidated most of their investments and emptied their safety deposit box. By the time she came to her senses, all that was left was the house.

She was furious.

The divorce was messy and she was extremely bitter by the time they faced each other in court two years later.

She was awarded half the house, which they had to sell in order to divide the asset.

Liz explained that she had bought a house with the proceeds of her divorce settlement and that this was the second home she had owned since she had been on her own. The profit she made when she sold the first one had enabled her to upgrade and buy into our neighbourhood.

I could relate to her independence. I also understood her strategy of buying and selling houses. What I admired most, though, was her ability to pull herself together after a bitter divorce and get on with her life.

Liz hadn't worked since university and had no marketable skills. The court awarded her alimony of $2,000 a month for five years. The judge stated that five years should give her sufficient time to take courses and become self supporting.

After two years of working at an art gallery, earning peanuts, she started to panic. There was no way, she said, that she would be able to provide a decent living for herself on the wages she was earning. But if she went back to school and finished her degree, which she abandoned to get married, it would still take time to build a career and make a decent income.

She said she began exploring jobs that provided the opportunity to earn good money, but with minimal training. She knew it was a tall order, but she investigated the real estate world, the securities industry, and even considered starting her own business.

She explained that she then met a woman who worked for a major stock brokerage firm. The woman, a top stock-broker, was looking for an assistant to help manage her client accounts. It was basically an administrative position, but Liz said she thought it would give her a chance to see whether or not she might enjoy working as an investment advisor.

Well, she loved it, she said, and a whole new world opened up for her. She learned so much. She loved helping the clients, met some very interesting people and created a whole new social life through her contacts. She immediately registered to take the required courses and successfully completed them within four months. After one year, she began dealing with the clients and after three years, her income was in the six figure bracket and she was on her way.

Liz explained that she then moved to a small brokerage firm as the director of sales and was granted the opportunity to buy stock in the company each year for 10 years. Two years ago, the company was bought by another firm and, as she quite candidly told us, she tendered her shares for three times the amount that she had paid for them.

It was quite a story. We were impressed, not that she was trying to impress us. She told her story in a matter-of-fact manner, which made us like her even more, and we felt a sense of pride for our new friend who had made it in the face of adversity.

We sat quietly, absorbing her story and then we related other tales of other women we knew who had ended up divorced. Most women get short-changed when it comes to divorce, especially ones with children. Someone said a recent statistic stated that if you were married in the past 20 years, you have a 50 percent chance of becoming divorced. And second marriages often end in divorce as well, because women tend to marry the same type of man again and find themselves in the same situation a second time.

The discussion continued for at least an hour and finally Ruth went to her house and came back carrying a bottle of wine. After three attempts, and adamantly refusing help, she uncorked it, and we toasted the success of our new friend.

We left the July meeting with a feeling of renewed vitality and, I might add, a little light-headed from the wine.

The August meeting brought yet another neighbour, Judy. Judy had, with her common-law husband Paul, lived in the neighbourhood for two years but we only saw her on occasion, saying hello as we passed. She was in her mid 40s and she explained that Paul travelled quite a bit on business as a salesman for a large company. She was thrilled to be invited, because she knew so few of the neighbours and was happy to finally get to know us. I could tell that Ruth was a bit uncomfortable at first with Judy, because Ruth didn't believe in common-law relationships.

Judy explained that she worked for a trust company which had just been taken over by a bank, and that her job had become quite stressful. She had been widowed 10 years ago and was left with two teenage boys who caused her a great deal of grief. The boys were both on their own now and she had sold the family home and moved in with Paul, whom she had been dating for years but delayed making a commitment to until the boys were established and she was on her own.

I saw Ruth relax a little as Judy related her story to us and I secretly smiled to myself as I watched my friend adjust to a modern situation.

An interesting discussion took place at our August meeting. Cathy told us about lectures she'd been attending all summer to help her improve her performance in the classroom. She explained that a new report had been published in the U.S. that accused teachers of creating an unfair playing field for girls in the classroom and she found the report very offensive.

This report apparently revealed that boys receive more attention than girls do in class and are encouraged to excel, and that girls are denied certain opportunities. This gender bias makes it impossible for girls to receive an education equal to the education boys receive.

I said that I thought that there was merit in that statement as I couldn't remember any boys sitting on their hand and being force to write right handed.

Cathy continued to explain that the report indicated that teachers are unaware that they are transmitting sexist messages, so each day an individual teacher taught to a classroom of other teachers who pretended that they were back in the sixth grade. They were stopped every time the counsellors saw an example of biased action.

"But today so many more women are entering fields that they never did before," Annie said. "I think that the report must be outdated. We have women doctors, scientists even engineers. How do you explain that Cathy?"

"I would venture to say that some women have the natural ability to break through the system, but for the most part the school system is still functioning as it did years ago. I didn't realize that I was biased and it certainly isn't anything that I did consciously. But I was taken to task a few times during the session because of my apparent lack of attention toward the girls. I guess that what I was doing was overseeing the boys more, because they seem to get out of control in the classroom."

"If I'm hearing you correctly, you are saying that because the girls are quiet and well-behaved, they lose out on the teacher's attention," Ruth said.

"Yes, that is exactly what I am saying."

"You know," I said, "what you are relating really makes sense to me, because whatever it is that creates this problem, that is, women not standing up for their rights, has to be widespread and if it is created or enhanced in the school system, it explains why the problem is so prevalent."

"I believe that it begins in the home," Cathy said.

"Where the mother should be," Ruth slipped in.

"Look. In today's world, it isn't feasible for the mother to stay home. Her income is needed just to survive," Annie stated. "Without my additional income, Mark and I would not be able to afford our home."

"Maybe your lifestyle is out of whack," Ruth said pointing her finger. "When we first started out we couldn't afford a home. We rented for 10 years before we saved enough money to buy a house and then the next 15 years were spent paying off the mortgage. You young people today want to have it all, now, and because you are under so much pressure it is the children who suffer."

"I don't think that this situation has anything to do with a mother working," Cathy broke in. "It is more a function of our upbringing right from the cradle. As soon as they wrap that pink blanket around us, we are in trouble."

And so it went, each meeting dealing with different issues. We learned about and from each other and realized that no matter what our situation in life, we were not the only ones with problems. Some of the meetings were more social than educational - sometimes we just chatted away about day-to-day things that affected our lives.

The September gathering was once again at Annie's house. We had been discussing the dreaded up-coming season earlier, and this conversation was fresh in our minds as we basked in the sun. Winter, so cold and bitter, was rapidly approaching. Slipping, sliding, the slush, the wind, heavy coats and boots. The longer we lingered, the cooler it got, until the sun finally disappeared behind the trees and a chill sent us scrambling for warmth. The phone rang just as we came through the door and Annie ran to answer it.

Mark, who had taken Brett out for the day to allow Annie some free time, came in behind us. The startled tone in Annie's voice caused me to take Brett out of his father's arms to enable him to go to her. Then everything fell apart.

There had been some sort of accident and by the sound of the conversation, the situation wasn't good. Annie was crying and Mark had taken the phone and was busy writing information on a pad near the phone. Ruth instinctively put the kettle on and the rest of us finished cleaning up while we waited for Mark to get off the phone. Annie was near hysterics and Ruth comforted her, but we couldn't understand what she was saying through the tears and sobbing. Mark hung up the phone and sat down beside Annie and held her. The sobs lessened as he explained that Annie's father had suffered a stroke in Arizona and was in very poor condition. As Annie was an only child, her mother wanted her to fly to Arizona.

It was then that Ruth stepped in. She said, "Mark, you take Annie up stairs and get packed. Liz, you call the airlines and get them a flight. Then go get your car. You can drive them to the airport. Barb," she said to me, "get in touch with Mark's partner, the number is on his business card, and tell him Mark will be away. Judy and Cathy, go to your bank machine and get as much cash as you can, they'll need it. I will watch Brett until they make a decision about what to do with him."

Ruth took charge like an army sergeant and within an hour we had all completed our assigned duties. We met back in the kitchen, where she had just finished feeding Brett. Ruth concluded that what we had accomplished was satisfactory.

Annie and Mark came down the stairs with two suitcases and were told that a flight had been arranged in an hour and a half. Ruth handed them $600 in cash, which could be converted into U.S. dollars at the airport, and volunteered to baby-sit Brett until they returned. We wished them good luck as Liz drove them away.

We'd been caught up in a small whirlwind of activity for the past hour, and after they left Cathy, Ruth, Judy and I sat down to sip the fresh pot of tea Ruth had prepared.

"Wow," I said, "life changes so rapidly."

"I can't believe how our nice afternoon shifted to such a crisis in no time flat," Judy exclaimed.

"Well Ruth, you've got your job cut out for you until they get back," I said, as we watched Brett empty all the pots and pans from a cupboard. "He's beautiful, but he is a two-year-old. Are you sure you can handle him?"

"I'll help," said Cathy, "I'll spell you off from 5:30 until, say, 7:30 in the evening. That'll give you a little time to yourself to let you catch your breath."

"That's great," said Ruth. "I'll probably be standing at the door waiting for you - I'm not as young as I used to be."

I said, "Well, Ruth, you better find out who and where the baby-sitter is, and tell her what's going on."

"Oh, my goodness, in all the confusion, I forgot that he goes to the baby-sitter," Ruth said placing her hands on the sides of her head. "How am I going to get him there and back?"

The phone rang. We froze, fearing the worst. Finally, on the fourth ring, Judy picked it up. It was Annie on the car phone.

"Thank you," the sobbing little voice said. "Thank you so much."

Chapter Two
October

The nip in the air forced us to pick up our pace as we made our way, heads lowered to protect us from the bitter wind, towards Liz's house. Our footsteps made crunching noises on the fallen leaves as we walked down the street.

We were all anxious to see Annie. We knew that she and Mark had returned from Arizona after one week, but we had no details, except that her father had been transported by plane to a hospital here, and that his condition had not improved. I had only spoken to Ruth once since their return. She was completely exhausted after her week with Brett and even though Cathy and I had helped a bit, I know it had taken her two weeks to recover. Now Ruth was perky again, so I knew that she was rested.

Liz greeted us at the door and we entered her world. By the time our jackets were hung up, we had had a pretty good view into the three rooms which centred off the main entrance. Not one of us spoke. It was breathtaking!

Who would have guessed that she would be partial to a Chinese motif? The rooms were decorated completely in black and white with red accent pieces strategically placed throughout.

We felt as though we had left Canada and entered China through a magic looking glass, which we missed when coming through the doorway.

Finally Judy caught her breath and exclaimed, "Oh, Liz, this is perfect," and with that we all headed in different directions to inspect unusual pieces which caught our eye. We continued our investigation until the doorbell rang and Annie entered. We watched her go through the same routine. We realized how silly we must have looked, as she stood with her mouth open, peering into the room trying to absorb everything at once. We laughed and gathered on a white circular couch in front of a black marble fireplace, which was beckoning us with its dancing flame.

"I thought a nice warm saki would take the chill off us," Liz offered.

"Great idea," I said, "and it will give us time to take in your beautiful home. Thank you."

Liz brought a tray of drinks and we started to relax and talk. She explained that she had attended a conference a few years ago in Hong Kong and had fallen in love with the country and its people. She purchased thousands of dollars worth of pieces and upon her return, discarded all of her old furniture and redid the main floor of the house. We were looking at the result.

"I didn't realize that you were such a world traveller, Liz," I said.

"I go abroad every opportunity I can. Besides enjoying travel, I found, when I was working, that travelling educated me and provided a better perspective for some of the investment programs that I put in place for the firm."

"You mean you bought investments for clients overseas?" I asked, curiously.

"Not directly. We encouraged the account executives to diversify their clients' portfolios through investments that specialize in foreign markets," she explained.

"Oh, wow, over my head," I said, "it's all I can do to keep track of the Canadian real estate market without watching what is happening around the world."

"We can't all be versed on everything. I know little about the real estate market, Barb. By visiting different places, I realize how small Canada is in the world scheme of things. There is so much going on elsewhere and it is fascinating to be exposed to it. Every time I visit a different country I come back with a better concept of how the world functions. Each country has something different to offer, yet their basic needs are the same."

"I envy you, Liz," Cathy said. "I've never been outside of Canada. Come to think of it I've never been outside Ontario, yet I teach history and geography. Somehow that doesn't make sense."

"Travel is one of the easiest ways to broaden your knowledge. You experience different cultures, explore historical sites, and see first-hand the effects of economic and political policies and the problems that accompany them. In addition to that, I can order coffee, buy shoes, and find the bathroom in six different languages," Liz laughed, as she offered more saki.

The foreign drink was working. There wasn't a chill for several feet in any direction. As we settled in and the chatter eased, our thoughts turned to Annie.

"Please tell us about your dad, Annie, how is he?" Liz asked.

"Oh, it is such a disaster story that I hardly know where to begin," she said, taking a sip of her drink. "First of all, his stroke was severe and in all likelihood he won't recover. He is on life-support systems and has not recognized anyone or spoken for three weeks. I guess we have resigned ourselves to the fact that we are going to lose him, that it is just a matter of time.

"The problems we faced, the mechanics of moving him and trying to straighten out the financial situation, just added to the burden and my mother is just about at her wit's end."

"What do you mean?" Judy asked.

"Well, she is staying with us. She has no home and no money." With that Annie started to cry.

"Start at the beginning, Annie, and take your time. We have all afternoon," Judy prompted.

She took another sip of her saki and began.

"My mother never worked outside the home, and she left all of the financial matters to my dad. When dad retired, they sold their home and bought a motorhome. This is something that they had always wanted to do, travel the United States, see the Grand Canyon, all of the mid-west, and ultimately drive up the coast of California and British Columbia to Alaska."

She stopped to wipe her nose.

"They left in July and were gone only two months when dad had the stroke," she continued. "He was admitted to a hospital in Tucson and was very well cared for. They really did a good job. The day the phone call came was actually the third day of his hospital stay. Mom didn't want to upset me until she found out how serious his condition was."

"I can understand that," Ruth said.

"Yes, I don't have a problem with that either. I probably would have done the same. I can't imagine what she was feeling, though. The RV park where they were staying was about thirty miles from the hospital and Mom tried to rent a car to make it convenient for her to travel back and forth to the hospital."

"What do you mean, 'tried'?" Judy asked.

"Apparently, you can't rent a car unless you have a credit card and they wouldn't accept Dad's. Mom never has had one. She told them that she could pay cash. They said that they were sorry, but they had to have a credit card, so she took a cab back and forth. She went to the hospital every day at eight in the morning and stayed until eight at night. She called us after the administration of the hospital explained that there was a problem with their medical coverage. Apparently, because Dad had been taking high blood pressure pills, which were prescribed for him within three months of the stroke, the insurer claimed that he had a pre-condition, which nullified their medical coverage. That's when she called us to help get him back to Canada. At least here, his medical bills will be covered, but he stayed 10 days in the U.S. hospital which cost $28,000 U.S. and the provincial insurance paid less than $2,000."

"What did you do?" Cathy asked, horrified.

"Mark called his partner, who went to the bank and borrowed

the money which he then wired to us. Could I have more saki, please, Liz? This is really a long story and it gets worse," she explained, holding her glass up to be refilled.

"Mark's brother flew to Tucson and drove the motorhome back. Thank God for the help of everyone. I don't know what we would have done if we hadn't had a network of wonderful friends and relatives to help and support us through this. Did I thank you?" she asked.

"Yes, you did. Go on with your story," I said.

"Well, we don't have that kind of money. We are just lucky that our bank manager knew us fairly well and we have always paid our bills. He understood the situation and based on the business assets, he lent us the money. The plan was to sell the motorhome, which is worth about $100,000, when we got it back to Canada and pay back the bank. When Mom and Dad sold their home, they paid cash for the RV and put the rest of the money in a term deposit at the bank."

"That was good thinking, Annie," Judy said.

"The plan would have worked, except that the motorhome is in Dad's name and we can't sell it."

"But you have the term deposit," Liz reminded her.

"That's in Dad's name as well." With that, she broke down and sobbed.

Ruth moved closer to Annie and put her arm around her shoulders and held her while she tried to compose herself.

The rest of us sat in silence.

"Dad receives a pension cheque every month and that is being deposited into a bank account in his name and my mother can't even get spending money."

"My God, how can this happen?" Cathy demanded to know. "Doesn't the bank understand the situation?"

"Certainly they do, but it is out of their hands," Annie replied.

"That's right! The bank can and certainly will help, but they have to work within the law," Judy explained. "This is why it is so important to have all banking assets registered jointly allowing both access. It eliminates problems like this."

"Annie, your dad must have a will," Ruth said, searching her mind to offer a solution. "Find it and it'll probably show that your mother is entitled to everything."

"Good thinking, Ruth," Cathy reinforced. "Have you found the will, Annie?"

"Hang on," Judy said. "A will does not come into effect until someone dies, and Annie's father is not dead. Most people believe that they are safe and secure if there is a will, but it certainly will do nothing in a situation like this."

"What now?" I said. "Judy you work for a trust company. What happens?"

"Well the law is currently changing and for the better, I might add. Today, you must apply to the court for what is called a committeeship, which is a lengthy, expensive process.

However, shortly you will only have to have a person declared mentally incapable and then a family member can become the guardian of his property by applying through the Public Trustee's office."

"Do you have a lawyer, Annie?" Cathy asked.

"No," she replied. "We don't."

"No problem! A good friend of mine is an excellent lawyer specializing in trust law," Cathy said, as she threw her jacket over her shoulders. "I'll slip home and get his card for you and you can call him first thing in the morning."

"Annie, it's a blessing that your mother has you. What ever would she do if she were alone?" Ruth asked.

"I don't know, Ruth. She asks that question every day. Go on welfare, I suppose," she responded.

"We had a client in one of our branches, in her 70s," Judy related. "Her husband wanted to take a trip to see a sister in Calgary and he wanted to drive. His wife didn't want to go with him and he set out alone. He was last seen in Winnipeg and never heard from again. His car and all his possession were recovered, but he was never found. All of their money was invested with my company, and all of it was in his name. The body was never found and the wife had to wait seven years, until he was declared legally dead, before she got a penny, and she was desperate."

My heart sank, and that feeling of loneliness came over me again. I hadn't experienced it in years and I sat quietly pondering what would happen to me if I was unable to take care of my affairs. I made a mental note to ask Cathy for her lawyer friend's phone number.

"Here's the card Annie," Cathy said as she returned to the living room.

"You will like him. We used him when my dad passed away and he is excellent."

"If your mother had a power of attorney, all of these problems would have been eliminated, Annie," Judy said.

"What's a power of attorney?" asked Ruth.

"Well, it's the right to act on behalf of another person," Judy stated. "My mother had Alzheimer's disease, and I was able, through the power of attorney which she granted me when she was well, to sell her Florida property, liquidate investments and provide her with the care which she was entitled to and deserved. A power of attorney is one of the most important, under-used legal instruments available in Canada."

"Where do you get a power of attorney form?" asked Annie.

"A lawyer can prepare one for you," Judy said. "You can obtain one from a bookstore, but I wouldn't recommend that. You must be careful who you grant the permission to, so you should have legal advice. But Annie, it is too late for your father to grant a power of attorney, unless he recovers."

"That is unlikely. I can't believe that I've never heard of a power of attorney before," said Annie.

"You know," Ruth said, "if anything happened to Bob, I would be in the same situation. I have no idea about our financial affairs. I wouldn't even know where to start. You have scared the devil out of me, Annie."

"Unfortunately, I saw this every day when I was working," Liz stated.

"Women are often uninvolved in the day-to-day financial affairs of the family and when something happens to their spouse, they are totally in the dark."

"A woman I worked with and her husband took a weekend trip to New York, through the Finger Lakes region directly south of Lake Ontario," Cathy recalled.

"They had a terrible accident and both ended up in the hospital. The medical bills were so large that they had to sell their house to cover them."

"That's horrible, Cathy. We scoot across the border all the time to shop and who ever thinks to get additional medical coverage for a day or a weekend," Judy said.

"There are a lot of things we don't think about until it is to late, and because of our trusting nature, I think women think of these things less than men," Ruth said.

"I think that situation is changing for women," I interjected. "Today's women are more financially aware than ever before."

"Yes, you are right to a certain extent, Barb," Liz stated, "but I follow statistics about women and their financial knowledge and although we make more money today than we ever have in the past and we are breaking through that glass ceiling in the corporate world, we still know very little about the financial world and its effects on us. There seems to be two levels of financial awareness: the woman who is extremely knowledgeable and at the other end of the spectrum, the woman who has limited knowledge. There doesn't seem to be a middle level yet.

"The statistics tell us that 67 percent of woman pay the household bills, yet 87 percent have little knowledge of how to invest or protect themselves from a financial crisis. Look at us in this room. There are six of us, and how many of us are knowledge-able about the financial world and how to protect ourselves?"

Judy was the only one who raised her hand. "My knowledge comes from my work at the trust company, but I only know the products that my company offers and it is my job to understand," Judy stated. "Personally, I have great concerns because of my common-law relationship and the fact that I haven't taken the time to protect myself. It worries me."

"So here we are," Liz pointed out, "two out of six of us have knowledge and we only have that because of our profession. When my husband left I was in the same boat, he took care of everything. If I'd known then what I know now, I would have come out of that divorce in a much better financial position."

"I often worry about Mark's business. If anything happened to him, I wouldn't be able to carry the financial responsibilities that we have. We would lose our house and have to start all over again. I don't make enough to carry us," Annie said. "It scares me."

"Why don't we know these things? We're not stupid," said Cathy. "I have some savings and a good pension, but beyond that, nothing. I didn't know about the power of attorney and I certainly will never have a lot of money unless someone leaves it to me in a will or I win a lottery. It appears that we just accept our fate."

"I think it all goes back to when we were born," I said. "We were groomed and programmed from the beginning: our fathers protected us and encouraged the boys to be aggressive, preparing them for the role of provider. Our mothers encouraged this thinking because that's what they were taught. This scenario may have been fine years ago, but it leaves us less than prepared for the paths that women find themselves taking today."

"You're right, Barb," Cathy stated. "Remember that exercise I went through this summer? The facilitators explained to us that by the age of 11, girls are so affected by the boys' aggression that they begin to retreat and become passive. Apparently the problem is being viewed so seriously that some school systems are looking to segregation. Only this time, it is the boys from the girls. The theory has been tested and it has established that girls do much better academically and in sports when they are not subjected to the male environment."

"That's just great," Annie piped up. "Now that we are through with the school system and are struggling to survive, what do we do? It'll take 25 years for that to filter through the system, so our children or grandchildren will benefit, but where does that leave us?"

"I guess we'll have to educate ourselves," I said. "The women's movement has encouraged us to stand firm, to stand up for our rights, to fight for job and pay equity, and today, women are making more money than ever before, but we've never been taught how to manage it. Saving and investing for our future has not been a priority for us. Maybe what we are witnessing here is the start of the next stage of the women's movement."

"Ruth, you've been very quiet, what are your thoughts?" Cathy asked.

"I'm terrified," she said. "I've been reflecting on Annie's mother's situation and I have a sense of panic that I can't shake. I feel like I have to rush home and sit down with Bob and ask him to explain our financial situation to me in complete detail, immediately. I am very nervous."

"Don't be nervous, Ruth. You are ahead of the game, if that is what you are planning to do. You are not in a crisis situation and may never be, but at least you are going to head one off, if you follow through with your thoughts," Liz said.

"I don't even know where to begin," Ruth said, throwing her hands in the air. "He'll think I'm crazy if I start asking questions after all these years. I've never shown any interest before."

"Maybe he'll welcome the opportunity. It must be a burden to be totally responsible for the well-being of the family," Liz commented.

"Or maybe he'll resent my questions and tell me to mind my own business," Ruth replied.

"Well, I guess you won't know until you try," I said.

"Where do I begin?" she asked, looking up to the ceiling.

"You know," Liz said, "I've been thinking as we've been talking, especially after your comment, Barb, about the women's movement. What if we took our monthly meetings and spent an hour or two learning about our finances? I would be willing to guide you and help you put your financial houses in order. After all, this is what I did for a living."

"I thought you worked for a stock broker. I don't think I want to buy stock," Cathy said.

"I was licensed in the beginning of my career, but for the last 10 years, my role was one of educator, first learning about the financial products available and then helping the sales force understand them, and they in turn helped their clients," Liz explained. "We focused on financial planning through good sound investment strategies, which included mutual funds, and we specialized in registered retirement products."

"What's a mutual fund?" Ruth asked.

"I rest my case! I think it would be fun to explore the world of investments with you and hopefully over the winter months, you'll acquire enough knowledge to start you on your way to financial security."

"I think that is a wonderful idea," I said. "We'll start our own financial consciousness-raising group. I have been buying Canada Savings Bonds for 10 years and this year with interest rates so low, I don't know what to do, and they are going on sale in a few weeks."

'This is really nothing new, you know. Women have been getting together for years to invest money through investment clubs," Liz stated.

"They have?"

"Sure. Each month they put money into an account and they buy an investment together. They become members in the Canadian Shareowners Association. It teaches people how to evaluate a company and find one which, hopefully, will grow and then the club buys stock with their pooled money. They don't buy a lot of stock in any one company, but they may own the shares of four or five companies, depending on how much money they have in the account. Each month they study together and make their investment decisions, and based on a majority vote, they buy or sell their selected investments. We had many investment clubs who dealt with our firm."

"I think that's a marvellous idea - they learn together," Judy said.

"That's right. They make mistakes sometimes, but if they've done their homework properly, more often than not, they make money."

"How do we get started, Liz?"

"If we all agree that this is an exercise that you want to pursue, I think the first thing we had better do is start gathering information. Ruth, I am going to give you a list of things to talk to Bob about. You have already learned about the power of attorney, which, I think you should investigate as soon as possible. I recently gave my sister my power of attorney and it helps me sleep at night. Also, you should enquire about all your investments, who they are with and where the certificates are located. Prepare a list. Actually, what you should be doing is creating a net worth statement."

"How do we do that, Liz?" Cathy asked.

"A net worth statement is a list all of your assets on one side of a sheet of paper and opposite that, all of your debts. The difference between the two will give you your net worth. You should list everything you own and consider to be an asset. An asset would be anything that you feel has value and that could be liquidated, such as jewellery, cars, furniture and most of all, don't forget your house. When you list your debts, include your mortgage, outstanding car payments, credit card debt and personal loans that you may have."

"That won't take me too long," Cathy said. "I don't have much in the way of investments but I don't owe much either, except for the mortgage."

"That's good, but it is a necessary exercise to go through in order to establish how much more you'll need if and when you retire. Also, you want to be able to understand any insurance policies that you may have and to review the details of your and/or your husband's company pension plan," Liz continued. "You also need to know if there is a safety deposit box, where it is, and what it contains. Ruth, as well as you, Cathy and Annie, find out if your husband has a will prepared. You should know where all the banking is done and what loans are outstanding. If there are any Registered Retirement Savings Plans find out where they are and what they are invested in. If anybody owes you any money, this would be listed as an asset."

"This seems like a lot of work, Liz," Ruth said.

"I think that you'll be surprised how quickly you can prepare a complete statement. It really shouldn't take long at all," Liz reassured her. "Also, I want each of you to call Health and Welfare Canada - you'll find the number in the blue pages of the telephone directory-and ask for a statement of your Canada Pension Plan. Ask for one for your husband as well. This will help explain one of the reasons women live below the poverty line after retirement."

"I'll bring information from work about wills and estates, investments and RRSPs, Liz," Judy said.

"That's good, Judy, and because your company has been bought by a bank, maybe you could gather the information that they provide as well. It'll give us a good comparison. I will also call my former company and ask for information that we'll need, and bring it to our November meeting."

"It occurs to me that we are fortunate to have someone who was involved in the investment world as a friend. How do other people get this information?" I asked.

"Well, most people work with a financial advisor but this information is available to the public and it's just a matter of taking the interest, going into these institutions or calling them and asking for the material. Some people find the task over-whelming and unless they have a lot of time, it never gets done. You've heard that commercial on TV that states that people spend more time planning their annual vacation than planning their finances," Liz explained.

"Yes, I've heard that commercial and you know it is so true," Judy agreed.

"We are going to change that, and one of the things I would like you to do, Barb, is to call the stock exchange and talk to their public relations department. They'll be pleased to send a com-plete investor information package - ask for six packages - which we will use to help us understand how the stock market works. This is one of the first steps in our educational process. In fact, if you have the time and money, call The Montreal Exchange, The Alberta Stock Exchange, which is located in Calgary and The Vancouver Stock Exchange, as well as The Toronto Stock Ex-change. We might as well cover them all."

"Why do we have to start with the stock exchange?" ques-tioned Cathy.

"Because the stock market is one of the backbones of the financial world and I think you must have a basic understanding of how the markets work in order to make informed decisions when investing," Liz explained. "One of the biggest mistakes investors make is purchasing an investment blindly. Not understanding how the markets work can erode a portfolio quickly."

"We certainly don't want to start off on the wrong foot, do we," Ruth commented.

"No we don't, and I think that you'll find that there is nothing more satisfying than taking control of your own destiny," Liz said supportively.

"Yes, I agree totally. Liz, given what we are doing, what should I do about buying Canada Savings Bonds in November?" I asked.

"I would go ahead and buy them, Barb. It'll take us at least until January to begin to get a handle on the different options we have and you'll receive interest in the meantime if you don't cash them until January, so you have nothing to lose at this point."

"This is so exciting, I can't wait to get started," Ruth said.

"You know, this reminds me of the '60s," I said. "Women got together in small groups, not unlike this one, and discussed their situation. The numbers of groups increased and associations were formed, until they became quite a force to contend with. Everyone became more aware and much more knowledgeable about the issues which affected us - not only women but men, children, the government, and corporations. I think that this is the beginning of a new era for women."

"Financial awareness for women: networthing. I think this is great," Annie quipped.

"What I like about the concept," Cathy said, "is that we'll do it together, we will learn together. I would never do this on my own, but doing it as a group or a team, I am looking forward to the winter. It'll make the cold winter weather more bearable."

"Yes, it will," Liz agreed, "but if you want to do it properly, you'll have some reading to do. I suggest that you start by buying, even once a week, a financial newspaper, which will introduce you to the financial markets. Also, there are many TV programs that focus on financial matters. Go through the TV listing and then watch one. We are about to open a whole new world to you. It isn't necessary for you to understand the complete inner workings of the investment world, but you do have to have an idea about how certain actions and information affect your investments."

"Give us an example, Liz," Annie suggested.

"One of the areas which affects all of us is interest rates. Are rates high or low, where are they going, how long have they been at the current level? People who don't understand what happens when interest rates start to rise can make serious mistakes if they buy the wrong investments at the wrong time. It can be very costly. The problem with interest rates is that you and I can't control them so we must be in a position to take advantage of them when they head in a different direction," Liz explained.

"That is so true. I remember in the early '80s when interest rates were 20 percent," Judy said, "we had a mortgage which came due and the rate was so high that it almost doubled our payment and we were really struggling. It was then that my husband became ill and I had to go back to work, just to keep the house. We put it up for sale, but nobody wanted to buy it. We were living in Windsor, Ontario then. My husband worked for Chrysler and they almost went out of business. It was a terrible time. Three of our closest neighbours lost their homes and their jobs. Friends of ours who worked for Chrysler were offered early retirement packages, and some of them have never recovered financially."

"That is exactly what I am talking about. Interest rates are probably the critical factor, which is why it is important for us to understand how they work and how they affect us financially," Liz responded. "I am so pleased that you are interested in pursuing this. Some of the published statistics are very frightening. They state that only three out of 100 women will be financially secure at age 65."

"Why is that, Liz?" asked Annie.

"I suspect, just as someone said earlier, that most of us just accept our fate, instead of trying to make a change. We don't insist, when we are in a relationship, that the financial information and the planning include us," Liz said.

"That, coupled with the fact that it is so difficult for young people to think far into the future and start planning today," Ruth added.

"Not for me!" Annie responded. "This situation with my parents has really made me stop and think."

"It's unfortunate that it takes a crisis before things start falling into perspective," Liz replied. "Annie, you are the one who'll benefit the most from our sessions, because you are the youngest. Time is an important factor when planning your future. If you begin investing when you are young, you can start with a small amount of money, and if you continue to put a little bit aside every month without fail, by the time you are ready to retire, you'll have quite a nest-egg. But if you wait until you are older, as most people do, you run out of time and are forced to put a greater amount of money away in order to reach the same goal."

"Time has always been a problem for women. When you're a teenager, you want to be older, when you're in your 20s and 30s, there is never enough of it and when you get to be my age," Ruth said, "you want to be younger and you realize that you are running out of time."

"Ruth, you sound just like my mother," I said.

"You're right though, Ruth, and I think we've run out of time. It's 5:30. I can't believe how fast today has gone. I have to go. Brett will be ready for his dinner," Annie said.

"Let's just take a minute and go over what is to be done for next month," Liz said. "Ruth, you are going to look into the power of attorney."

"I am as well," Cathy interjected. "My mother isn't well and she is alone. I'm going to talk to her about giving me power of attorney, so if anything happens, I'll be able to handle her affairs."

"That's great, Cathy," Liz said. "You are all going to list all of your assets, insurance policies, bank accounts, RRSPs, investments, any loans, and all the contents in your safety deposit boxes. Don't forget your houses - for some people it is the biggest asset they have. Subtract what you owe from what the asset column shows and that'll determine what you are worth."

"I'm going to call the stock exchanges and get six investor information packages," I said.

"And don't forget to call Health and Welfare Canada and get an updated statement of your Canada Pension Plan," Liz reminded everyone.

"I feel better already. Somehow just putting the start of a plan together gives me comfort," Ruth stated.

"Good luck with Bob, Ruth, and we'll see you at your house in November."

Chapter Three
November

Ruth was busy putting the finishing touches to the most incredible canapes when we arrived. We were all bundled up: hats, boots and gloves. The snow had arrived early and we were all grumbling as we struggled to remove the layers of clothing.

Walking into Ruth's house was like taking a step back in time. She is a collector and it seems as though over the years she had purchased every expensive piece of china ever produced. Each corner had a shelf, proudly presenting her treasures, each one of them competing for attention.

"Ruth, you must spend all of your time dusting and polishing," Cathy said.

"If there is one thing that I excel at, it is polishing," she replied.

We settled in the family room and Ruth carried in a tray covered with hors d'oeuvres fit for a queen. In addition she had prepared a shrimp dip which was probably the best that I've ever tasted.

"Ruth you have outdone yourself. I vote for all our meetings to be at Ruth's," I stated, looking for supporters.

"I agree," said Cathy, selecting one of each hors d'oeuvre and placing them on her plate.

"Do you think that Annie will join us?" I asked.

"Yes," Ruth said. "She called last night to say she would be here. She felt that a few hours out of the house would take her mind off things."

Annie's Dad had passed away the week before. We had all attended the funeral, but we still wrestled with a sense of frustration at our inability to ease our friend's pain.

"She was really close to her Dad, wasn't she, Ruth?" Judy inquired.

"Yes, being an only child, I think, is additionally hard. The responsibility of making the right decisions was solely hers. Her mother simply wasn't capable. She had a hard time even deciding which casket to select."

The doorbell rang and Ruth let Annie in. The stress really showed on her. Generally, she was so vibrant, but the sleepless nights and pressure of her father's death were reflected in her face.

Ruth helped her with her coat and stood talking with her for a minute before she came in. Annie looked drawn and pale, but she entered the room with a smile and curled up on the couch.

"I'm glad to be here. It's been a rough couple of weeks and I really need a diversion," she stated.

"Well," I said, passing her the tray of treats, "hopefully, you'll now be able to get back to some sort of schedule and over time, life will become normal again for you. How is your mother holding up?"

"Oh, it's one thing after another," she murmured. "We were notified yesterday that Dad's pension cheques will stop next month."

Ruth almost dropped the tea pot. "What!" she exclaimed, as she grabbed the spout to steady the pot.

"Apparently, when Dad arranged his pension, he chose a higher monthly payment, rather than provide an income for my mother after he died," she related.

"You mean that she'll receive no pension?" Ruth asked in horror.

"That's right, she signed a waiver agreeing to it. The concept would have worked if Dad had outlived her, or if they had both lived a long time, but his pension cheque stops next month."

"Why would she agree to such an thing?" Ruth asked in disbelief.

"Well, she said she didn't understand, and when Dad asked her to sign, she signed. He felt that they could better use the larger monthly amount. I don't even think that she considered the fact that he might die," Annie explained.

"What is wrong with us?" Ruth asked, shrugging her shoulders and shaking her head.

"I don't think there is anything wrong with us, I think there is something wrong with the rules that allow a situation like this to happen." Judy said emphatically. "Women, especially women who have never worked, should be entitled to the whole pension after the death of the husband until they die. The husband and wife should be treated as one. Or at least a survivor benefit should be mandatory for a spouse that has never worked. None of this signing away your benefits. When the form is received and a spouse has signed the waiver, the company should not accepted it unless it is witnessed by a lawyer who has taken the time to inform the woman of her rights and the consequences of her actions."

"Yes, the pension rules don't really address the responsibility to the non-working spouse," Liz said.

"What'll she do now, Annie?" Ruth questioned.

"She'll be living with us. Actually, it may work out well. Next week she starts looking after Brett and I eliminate the cost of my baby-sitter. My mom is very active and I think she'll be able to handle him. It'll also save us money, not to mention time."

"It'll probably be good for her as well," Ruth interjected.

"Yes, it will keep her mind off my Dad, who she misses terribly, and I'll be able to leave the house almost an hour later in the morning which will make my life much easier," Annie said trying to find something good in the situation.

"That makes a lot of sense, Annie," I said.

"What are you going to do with the motorhome?" Ruth asked.

"Dad had a will and we were able to transfer the vehicles and term deposit to Mom, as well as Dad's bank account. The motorhome is up for sale, but nobody wants to buy a motorhome in November, although, Mark's brother, who drove it home, is interested, but not until the spring. We just take one day at a time. No use worrying. We can't change the situation."

"Good approach Annie," Liz said, trying to change the topic because Annie looked ready to cry. "Speaking about approaches, Ruth, how did you get along with Bob when you asked him about your finances?"

"Well, surprise, surprise! I cooked his favourite meal and had the fireplace going, but after dinner when I served the lemon meringue pie, he knew something was up," she related.

"You mean that old trick still works?" I said. "You can still get to men through their stomachs?"

"Doesn't work on mine," Cathy said. "I guess because I'm not a very good cook."

"I told him about our last meeting and all the problems that Annie's mother was having and we just started to talk. He was actually surprised that I was taking an interest, and over that following week, every night, he explained what we had and where everything was located. We made a list of all our investments. On Wednesday, we went to the bank and documented everything in the safety deposit box, on Friday he arranged a meeting with a lawyer, and tomorrow we sign power of attorney forms."

"Wow!" Annie exclaimed. "You certainly have been busy."

"That's not all. I told him that Liz was going to teach us how to invest and before I knew it, he wrote a cheque and gave it to me to invest. He said that if I didn't lose it in the market, he'll let me take over managing our investments.

"I've been reading a financial newspaper and every Saturday night we've been watching a television program on investing. I am confused, but I find it fascinating and I have a thousand questions for you, Liz."

"Ruth, you are going to be my prize student, and I'm thrilled with what you have accomplished in such a short time," Liz said. "Barb, did you get the information from the stock exchanges?"

"Did I?" I said. "I called the Monday morning after our last meeting. The people were really great and within a week I had six packages. I have so much information here that I think they must have sent six of everything they've ever produced. As you said, Liz, this is a whole new world for us."

"I think, rather than spending the time it would take to sift through the information here, let's all take a package home and read it. It'll make more sense after we have spent the afternoon talking about the markets. If, when you go through the information, something is not clear, make a note and we will deal with the questions at next month's meeting," Liz said, as she handed each one of us a package. "We have a lot of ground to cover, so let's begin. I want to ensure, as we progress, that you understand the basics of how the markets work, what drives them and what affects them. Most investors buy and sell at the wrong time and hopefully once we have covered the basics, you'll avoid that pitfall. I'll focus on The Toronto Stock Exchange, because it is Canada's largest. If you have any questions as I go through it, just stop me and ask. Let's have a good understanding in the beginning and that should eliminate any confusion in the future."

"It all seems very confusing to me now," Cathy stated.

"Well, let's unravel it," Liz suggested. "It really is quite simple. Look, each one of you can drive a car, but are any of you capable of tearing the engine down and rebuilding it?" Liz asked.

"Not me! I call a tow truck if I have a flat tire," Annie said.

"It is the same thing with investing. You don't have to know the inner workings of the market - leave that to the experts, just as you do with your car. But you should know certain things or you won't be able to make informed decisions. Just think of this exercise as training for your driver's license, except that you'll end up capable of wheeling in and out of the markets."

"I don't think I'll ever understand," Cathy said.

"I suggest, Cathy, that you'll not be able to say that by the end of today. Actually, the stock exchange is a very busy and efficient organization, where millions of shares are bought and sold every day. It has to be orderly or at the end of the day it would be chaos, trying to figure out who bought and sold what.

"Let's establish first that a stock or share represents ownership in a company. A company raises money from the public, you and I, who buy their shares. This makes us part-owners in the company. These shares are then traded back and forth at different prices between thousands of investors through the stock exchanges. There are stock exchanges all over the world, but in Canada we have only four. The Toronto Stock Exchange, the TSE, as I mentioned is the largest in Canada and has the greatest number of shares of blue chip companies traded through it. Approximately 75 percent of all the shares traded in Canada are placed through the Toronto Stock Exchange."

"What is a blue chip company?" Cathy asked.

"A blue chip company is a large corporation that is well established and financially strong. Their shares are considered high quality. These major corporations have established an earnings track record and continuously paid dividends.

"The Montreal Exchange, the ME, is Canada's oldest exchange and is generally rated second in quality. The Vancouver Stock Exchange, the VSE, is known as the venture capital market, where small companies come to the public to raise funds to develop new products or ideas."

"Isn't that the risky one?" asked Judy.

"Well, historically it has had a bad reputation, but the securities commission has been working very hard over the past few years to clean it up through the introduction of new rules. It can still be risky, however, because quite a number of the companies listed on the VSE are new or focus on speculative areas, like mining exploration. If you buy a stock on the Vancouver exchange and the story is authentic and the company has sound management, you can make a lot of money. Conversely, you can lose a lot as well."

"That's the one I'll avoid," Cathy said. "I am afraid of losing my money. I remember Dad talking about the crash of '29."

"Everybody lost money then," Liz said, "but times have changed. Back in the '20s and '30s there weren't the controls in place as there are today. You don't have to buy stock listed on the Vancouver exchange, but some people I know, only buy risky stock. And always remember, the greater the risk the greater the potential reward.

"The Alberta Stock Exchange, the ASE, specializes in junior companies with an emphasis on oil and gas, as it is located in the heart of Canada's oilfields. There is also a commodities exchange in Winnipeg which deals only in the futures markets of mainly agricultural products."

"What do you mean by a commodity?" Ruth asked.

"A commodity is a raw product that is bought and sold through an exchange. Commodity trading began as a method for producers and manufacturers to lock in prices today, for delivery at some time in the future."

"You don't mean that investors actually buy something and take it away, do you?" Ruth continued with her questioning.

"No, and let's not refer to the participants in the commodity markets as investors. Except for the producers and users of the products, they are speculators, and these speculators never take delivery of what they have purchased through the commodities exchange. It is rather an exercise of betting on the rise or fall of future prices for a profit. If there is a shortage of coffee, it means that the price of coffee should rise, so the speculators purchase a futures contract which guarantees the price today. If the price rises they then sell their contract at a profit, before the delivery time."

"So speculators in commodities are not long-term investors. If prices go up, they make money, if prices decline they lose," Ruth said nodding her head.

"I've heard of pork-bellies. What other products are bought and sold through the commodities exchange?" Judy asked.

"I think that Ruth is speculating in china but she takes delivery of the commodity," Annie said, laughing.

"Yes, she could be, but her collection is probably very valuable. It is certainly more valuable than my collection of shoes," Liz replied. "I mentioned coffee, but they also trade in cocoa, sugar, barley, wheat, soybeans, vegetable oils, wool, tea, rubber and metals. In fact, there is a metals exchange in London, England, called the London Metal Exchange. It is this exchange that the rest of the world monitors, as this is where the exact price of gold is established, based on the trading throughout the day. We won't spend any time on the commodities markets as they are pure speculation or special purpose markets. Commodities are very risky and the prices fluctuate wildly. This is not an area for new investors like us. We are going to focus on investing. We'll focus on stock and mutual funds only."

"Can we visit any of the stock exchanges?" Ruth asked.

"Yes, you can," Liz replied.

"You can?" asked Cathy surprised. "I think that would be interesting. Perhaps I could arrange a field trip for my students."

"Yes, I believe you can. The Toronto exchange is located in the Exchange Tower, which is in the heart of the financial district of Toronto. You can arrange a tour, which is very informative, or go up to the viewing area overlooking the trading floor on your own. In fact, I would encourage you to do this, Cathy. If schools taught children about investing, we wouldn't be sitting here today.

"The Toronto Stock Exchange is actually a very colourful place. Different brokerage houses are represented by traders who wear distinctively coloured jackets."

"Why is that necessary?" Ruth questioned, as she poured us a fresh cup of tea.

"This tradition allows someone at a distance to identify which brokerage house is buying or selling a particular stock. It serves as a quick reference."

"I saw them on TV the other night," Ruth remembered. "I wouldn't be caught dead in public in one of these jackets. Some of them are very bright colours and loud plaids."

"My ex-husband would have fit right in," Cathy said.

"The floor is mainly dominated by men, still today. Traders are a breed unto themselves and very few women are comfortable working on the floor of the exchange."

"Maybe if women had been involved in the exchanges in the beginning, the traders would look more stylish," Judy quipped.

"Probably," Liz replied. "In addition to floor traders, all of the exchanges have sophisticated electronic communications to facilitate the timely trading of shares."

"What do you have to do in order to buy a stock, Liz?" Ruth asked.

"If you want to buy a stock, you must first open an account at one of the exchange member firms, of which there are more than 70 in the TSE."

"Is your former firm one of them?" Annie asked.

"Yes, they are one of the largest firms in Canada. Most of the securities firms in Canada are members. When you open your account the broker will ask you several questions about your financial situation - your net worth, how much money you earn, what your level of investment knowledge is, among other things. This is a regulatory requirement called the 'know your client' rule."

"Why do they need all this information, Liz?" Ruth asked. "It seems like an invasion of privacy."

"This information helps the broker understand which investments may or may not be appropriate for you and also whether or not you can afford to invest.

"You'll also have to tell them your age."

"Not me!" said Judy. "I haven't even told Paul my true age."

We laughed.

"Once your account is opened and you have placed your order, the sales executive will write up what is called a ticket, or in some larger houses, they'll enter your request directly into a computer. Your request is then transmitted to the firm's floor trader, who is located at the exchange. The floor trader walks your order to the trading post that represents the company whose stock you want to buy."

"You mean that there is a post stuck in the floor?" asked Cathy.

"Years ago it was a post, but today it is a designated area with a computer. I was just reading a story about how the trading post was established. Apparently in 1875 a trader broke his leg and was unable to move around, and the other traders had to come to him to trade specific stocks. The trader found this situation so profitable, that the tradition continued on after his leg healed and still does today."

"It seems to me that the stock exchange is big on tradition," Annie said.

"Yes, Annie, that is very true. The forerunner which ultimately became the New York Stock Exchange started in 1792. Any entity that began so long ago carries with it specific customs or rituals."

"I didn't realize that the act of trading securities began so many years ago. That's amazing," Ruth declared.

"That's right, and you thought that you had discovered something new," Liz laughed and continued. "At the stock trading post there will be another trader with an order to sell the same stock you want to buy and will hopefully sell it at the price you want to pay. The price is negotiated and your trader confirms your purchase back to the office of your broker," Liz explained.

"What if no one wants to buy your shares?" Judy asked.

"Well, someone will always buy your shares, not necessarily at the price you want to sell. The firms have a 'market maker' or a specialists who keeps the market going, and he is obligated to buy and sell to maintain a market price. The only time I experienced a problem was October 19, 1987. Nobody wanted to buy, only sell, so the prices kept going down until they were low enough to entice the buyers or the specialists at extreme discounts."

"Scary stuff," Annie said, shaking her head.

"It can be at times," Liz replied. "After the stock is purchased, the information is then fed into the computer and within a few days a confirmation statement will arrive at your home, advising you of the price and number of shares that you bought."

"You mean that you won't know for days whether or not you have actually acquired the stock?" Ruth asked.

"Not necessarily. If you ask your broker to call you when he has bought your shares, he can tell you, generally by the end of the day, whether or not he has a fill."

"Pardon. What's a fill?" asked Cathy.

"The security industry is full of buzzwords and you'll hear me use them. Sorry, it's just automatic. A fill means that the order has been completed as requested and your shares have been bought," Liz explained.

"You mean that you can buy stock without giving the broker money first?"

"Yes, but you must pay for your stock within five business days of the purchase. Once you are established with the broker, they'll place the order without cash in your account and ask you to mail in a cheque. This is another reason for the 'know-your-client' rule. The broker may not request the money until the settlement date if they are assured that you'll send in the money."

"That's generous of them and trusting," Annie commented.

"If you don't pay there can be serious ramifications. So I wouldn't try it."

"Is the whole industry computerized?" Judy asked.

"Pretty much. Some exchanges have switched to a completely computerized system and the floor of these exchanges is nothing more than a series of computers. Vancouver is one of them. It's a shame, actually, because it was an exciting place to visit with all the traders screaming and yelling orders. The prices were recorded on a series of blackboards, with young men walking around a ledge, making the price changes.

"The most exciting exchange that I have ever visited is New York. It's unbelievable. The noise, grown men shouting and the hand signals, as if their trying to wave down a fast moving train."

"Yes, I watched them on TV the other night. What does all that waving and gesturing mean?" Ruth asked, waving her hands in the air mimicking a trader.

"Each hand signal denotes a different meaning, such as price, number of shares or any important information that must be relayed quickly," Liz explained.

"Well, it is a sight to behold," Ruth said.

"There are more than 1,000 companies whose stock trades on the Toronto Stock Exchange and on a high volume day, it can be pretty hectic.

"Judy, your trust company was a publicly traded company when it was acquired by the bank. I owned shares in it, did you?" Liz asked.

"No, I didn't, but I wish I had, because the shareholders were offered $5 more than the price it was trading at on the day before the offer," she replied.

"Wow!" said Annie.

"This happens. Sometimes the best place to invest is in the company where you work. Often employees know whether or not their company is doing well and if the management is sound and effective. For example, Judy, if your company's mortgage department is busy with mortgage payment arrears and property repossessions, that would be a good indication that they are experiencing problems and I would hesitate to buy the stock. You may be privy to that type of information before the public. So in a lot of cases, the employees are more knowledgeable than the securities industry. But most employees don't look at their employer from an investment standpoint."

"You mean that if you work, let's say, in the automotive industry, and the company adds an extra shift, and interest rates are low and people are buying cars or trucks, especially after a recession when people have put off buying for a few years, you should be buying the company's stock?" Cathy asked.

"Certainly. Most investing is common sense. Another example is that famous shop that sells beauty products. We've all tried to get in those stores at Christmas time. You can hardly get through the door. It's quite a success story. So if you keep your eyes open and watch for a good idea and research it, you can do very well."

"I discovered that last week," Ruth said. "Bob has been buying his company stock through an employee stock purchase plan and in addition, he has bought shares directly in the market. He has all the faith in the world in his company, and because he works in the advertising department, he keeps track of the competition, constantly. Anyway, he has acquired quite a number of shares and at different prices, all lower than they are selling for today."

"That is a great strategy, Ruth. If you believe in your company and understand the market that they are in, it can be a great place to invest," Liz said.

"No wonder company executives live in such big expensive houses. They are exposed to everything the company is doing and probably have information that the workers or investors don't have, so they could make a killing by buying their own stock," Annie stated firmly.

"It is just not that easy, Annie. There are very strict rules that apply to officers and directors of listed companies and if they are caught buying or selling, based on information that the public doesn't have, they could go to jail, as it is illegal."

"How would we even know?" she challenged.

"Every key person at a listed company must disclose how many shares they hold and report to the securities commission every time they buy or sell their stock or any stock of a subsidiary. If a company has news or a new development, the public must be made aware promptly."

"I understand. But how would I know if they are buying or selling? It seems to me that if a president is selling shares in a company that they are operating, it would indicate that they don't have much faith in the company's future," suggested Annie.

"There is a report available to the public called 'Insider Trading' which is issued by the provincial securities commission.

And the newspapers often report who is selling and who is buying. It doesn't necessarily mean that the company is in trouble or the prospects for the future aren't good if senior people are selling. They may be selling for personal reasons. Maybe they are building a new home and don't want to borrow or they might be doing some tax or estate planning."

"I see. I guess you are right," Annie conceded. "But I would think that if a senior person is buying, it should be construed as a good sign."

"Yes, I would agree with you. When a company is analysed by the securities industry, they like to see key employees buying the stock. It is positive for the stock," Liz stated.

"Liz, I am confused. How does a stock originate?" Cathy asked.

"Well, it works through a process that is called 'going public.' Companies go public for a couple of reasons," Liz explained. "They may need to raise money to allow them to expand or to buy new equipment. They may want to increase their net worth, which will allow them to borrow more money, or maybe one of the founding shareholders wants to convert some holdings to cash. It can be a long process to sell the shares of a private company and a major shareholder may want to create a liquid interest in the company for estate purposes."

"But how do they get money for their shares?"

"A company can raise money from the public in two ways: either through debt, that is borrowing, or by selling part of the company to the public. These transactions represent two totally different approaches and it is important to distinguish between them."

"I suppose it is no different than when you buy a house. Most of us borrow from a lender - a bank, a trust company or a private individual - but you could also buy your house with a partner or a number of partners," Judy said. "Your house would then be owned by different people. If you borrowed from the bank, you would own your house free and clear when you paid the lender back. It is the same thing for a company."

"That's right, Judy. A company can borrow privately or publicly. If they choose to borrow from the public, they'll issue a bond, not unlike a promissory note repayable on a specific date at a specific price, the par value, which represents the principal amount borrowed, plus an interest rate which remains fixed, which they promise to pay you for the use of your money."

"Give us an example, Liz," Ruth requested.

"Let's say that a company we'll call International Manufacturing Corporation needs funds to expand their operation. The company would say to the investing public, 'if you lend us money, for five years, we'll pay you nine percent annually.' If the public thinks that International is going to be a safe investment, they'll lend them money. Each person may invest, for example, $10,000, and there may be thousands of investors. Each year, International faithfully pays the investors or lenders the interest, and the money they received helps them grow. But let's say four years later you need your money. International Manufacturing Corp. says sorry we made a deal and I don't have to pay you for another year."

"What do you do then, ask your neighbour to buy your bond?" Cathy asked.

"You could, and if you can find someone to buy your bond,

the purchaser will receive the interest for the remaining year and International will pay them the $10,000 at the end of that term. But let's say times have changed and interest rates are now currently 12 percent. No one would be interested in buying a bond that is only paying nine percent when they can lend another company their money and earn 12 percent interest."

"How do you get rid of the bond?" Ruth asked.

"You have to discount the value of your bond to make up the interest difference."

"You mean lose money?" Ruth questioned.

"Yes, let's assume that it is the anniversary date of the bond issue to keep it simple. By dropping the price of your bond from $10,000 to $9,900 which is a one percent drop the purchaser would receive nine percent interest plus one percent bond price reduction which equals approximately a 10 percent return. Not enough? We'll drop the price by three percent, which prices the bond at $9,700."

"That's a great way to make money," Cathy said sarcastically.

"Yes you'll lose money," Liz agreed. "But remember, you did earn the interest for the time you owned the bond and you have a capital loss for income tax purposes on the loss of your principal."

"I guess it doesn't make you feel any better, but at least you have your cash," Judy suggested. "And you couldn't have borrowed the money for one year at three percent."

"That's right," Liz said. "Remember we talked about interest rates last month and how they can affect your investments? When interest rates rise, bond prices fall. So the best time to buy a bond is when interest rates are high and as a result the bond prices are low. When interest rates fall, bond prices go up."

"My mind sees a teeter totter, you know, the kind the kids play on. When one end is up the other is down," Annie explained, moving her arms up and down.

"That's a great way to remember, Annie," I said. "But what if I can't find someone to buy my bond even if I discount it?"

"Well, one rarely sells a bond to a neighbour. Bond traders at brokerage houses spend their entire day putting sellers and buyers together. It is a huge market."

"Let me understand this," Cathy stated. "If when I wanted to sell my nine percent bond, interest rates had dropped to seven percent instead of going up, are you telling us that we would receive more money for the bond?" Ruth questioned.

"Yes, given our example of a two percent change in rates, you would receive approximately $10,200. The $200 is called a premium," Liz explained.

"So you really have to watch interest rates when buying and selling bonds," Ruth stated.

"No question, it is critical, unless you intend to hold the bond until maturity, at which time you'll receive the full value of the bond."

"How do we know if the company has the potential to pay us back at the end of five years?" Cathy asked.

"All publicly traded bonds are rated or graded, just like you teachers do with kids' work, in school. In fact one company uses an A,B,C rating formula, A, or better still AAA being attributed to the highest rated bonds."

"Who rates them, Liz?" I asked.

"There are two major bond rating companies in Canada. CBRS, the Canadian Bond Rating Service, and DBRS, the Dominion Bond Rating Service. These two companies continuously monitor all publicly issued bonds to ensure that nothing has changed within an organization, whether it be government or corporate, which would affect the quality of the bond and hence its quality rating. A rating is established when the bond is first issued and it is constantly watched. The rating may move up or down according to the information gathered by the rating companies. The rating also affects the price and interest rate of new bonds issued. The lower the rating, the higher the interest rate in order to attract buyers."

"We just went through an exercise similar to what you are saying, Liz," Cathy said. "Cal lent a friend $4,000 to help him out of a tough situation. The bank was unwilling to lend money to him as I guess that they felt he was a high risk. Anyway, he asked Cal for the money. We were nervous, afraid that we would never see our money again, but the fellow said he would pay us 15 percent interest. We had money coming due from a five year GIC and we could only earn seven percent if we renewed. Cal figured that the high return offered was worth the risk. We lent this friend the money for one year and he paid us back fully, plus the 15 percent."

"That was a very risky venture, Cathy, but you obviously weighed the pros and cons and were prepared to take the risk.

That is exactly how the bond market works," Liz confirmed.

"So where do we, the investor, get the ratings on these companies?" Ruth asked.

"Ratings are published regularly and your broker will be able to tell you what rating has been given to every bond in Canada."

"Is a poorly rated bond called a 'junk bond'?" Judy asked.

"Yes, they would have the lowest rating but offer the highest rate of return as they are extremely risky, not unlike Cathy's example. If that transaction could have been rated it would probably be considered a junk bond, especially because the bank had already refused to lend him the money. I keep repeating that the return and risk are directly related and nowhere is it more prevalent than in the fixed income market, that is, GICs, bonds and mortgages. If a bond is offered to the public at, say, 13 percent when current interest rates are at 11 percent, the higher interest rate should serve as a red flag warning you that this bond is riskier than one issued at the current rate. This rule is so fundamental to investing that it bears repeating - often. Investors who ignored this rule have experienced many problems over the past 15 years or so," Liz stated.

"In what way, Liz?" Cathy inquired.

"Well, a trust company would offer an interest rate to the public for GICs that could be anywhere from one-half to one percent higher than rates offered by other institutions. This meant that they needed money, and people rushed to give them their hard-earned cash, but then the trust company went into receivership and investors lost a lot of money. People have taken the word 'trust' in a company's name literally."

"But there is insurance for that," Judy stated.

"Yes, you are right. However if an investor deposited $60,000, which is the maximum amount covered today, for five years and the company experienced problems and was wound up in the fourth year, the investor would only receive $60,000, the original investment, with no interest. Also, it can take a long time to receive your money, in some cases up to a year or longer, unless you can prove hardship."

"I don't think anybody with $60,000 could plead poverty," Annie said.

"What if it was all the money you had in the world and you were retired, or maybe you only had $10,000 and needed it desperately," Judy stated.

"That's right, Judy, and there are situations where a receiver will release the money early, but it can be a hair-raising experience to have your money tied up and not be able to determine, immediately, the effects of the seizure. At least in the bond market you are generally liquid, that is, you can sell even if it is at a loss. There is an after market for GICs, although it is not as large as the bond market and liquidity is more of a problem."

"Liz, are bonds insured, like a GIC?" Ruth asked.

"No, but they are backed by the issuer, such as the Federal Government or a province that is borrowing, and if you buy a high grade corporate bond rated at AAA, you should have no fear about their ability to repay, if you keep an eye on their rating and make sure it isn't downgraded."

"Do you feel that you have a grasp on how the bonds work?" Liz asked.

"Yes I think we understand," Ruth answered.

"Yes, it really isn't that difficult, is it?" Annie replied.

"No, it isn't. There are two key things to remember when dealing in bonds. One: when interest rates rise, bond prices fall and when interest rates fall bond prices rise. Two: the greater the stated return, the higher the risk. If you keep these two thoughts in mind, you'll be able to invest in the bond market quite successfully," Liz reaffirmed.

"If you have no further questions, we'll venture into the stock side. Let's assume that our International Manufacturing Corporation needs more money. Their financial advisors tell them that they shouldn't borrow, but rather that they should sell part of their company to the public.

"The value of the company's assets and its past five year earnings record, plus the goodwill that the company has generated and the fact that their manufactured products are in high demand, place a $5 value on the stock."

"By listing the company, does it change the way they do things?" Judy asked.

"Yes, International will have to report to the new shareholders quarterly, and form a board of directors from inside and outside the company to represent the public shareholder's interest," Liz explained.

"That's good, someone to watch over the company's activities," I said.

"Yes, that's right. Let's assume that the company is very good at what they do and is well managed. This should make it an attractive stock in the market. They offer up 45 percent of the company which, we'll say, is worth $75,000,000 or 15,000,000 shares at $5 a share. This money flows into the brokerage firms from different investors, to be handed over to International, that is, after fees and expenses are paid. Everyone who helped the company get the new stock issue to the market must be paid. Lawyers, accountants, printers, and last, but not least, the brokers who were responsible for the successful distribution of the stock. For you see, when a new stock is issued, the investor pays no commission to the broker. It is the company, International, who pays the commission."

"What affects the stock's price after it is listed?" Annie asked.

"Supply and demand," Liz stated.

"What creates the supply and demand?" Annie inquired.

"Now that is the question! Generally speaking, many factors affect investor demand or lack of it. Current economic conditions, whether interest rates are poised to go up or down, how well the company is managed, whether or not it is profitable, or is likely to be more profitable in the future, whether or not there is room for growth in that particular industry, how much debt the company has incurred, whether or not earnings are sufficient to justify the current price, or whether the stock is undervalued."

"I guess supply and demand affects almost every transaction that takes places, doesn't it, Liz?" Judy commented.

"You bet it does. Take the oranges that we buy weekly at our local grocery store. Last January there was a major freeze in Florida, and most of the citrus crop was damaged, so the oranges that we've been enjoying cost double what they did last year. The supply of oranges can't meet the demand so up go the prices. We see this in everyday items, but accept it as part of life."

"Sounds to me like Economics 101," Annie said.

"Yes. Coupled with common sense," Liz interjected. "This is why, if you are interested in investing in a stock, a knowledgeable stock broker, one whose judgement you trust, is critical to your financial plan. It is also important that your advisor have access to a complete team of research people supporting and recommending different companies."

"Do all full service brokerage firms have research departments, Liz?" Ruth asked.

"Usually, yes. They have many research people behind the scenes. Each research analyst will have special knowledge in a specific area of the market. They study the market, the companies, interest rates, and all other conditions that may affect the price of the stocks that they follow."

"Can you ask to be put on the mailing list of these brokerage firms and receive this information?" Ruth wanted to know.

"Yes, you can. You can also subscribe to publications which are produced privately, by people who are analysts, but are not affiliated with any particular firm."

"Liz, I was watching a financial program on TV and at first I thought I had turned on a program about animals, what does 'bull and bear' mean?" Ruth inquired.

"I told you that the industry is full of buzzwords. It starts to make sense after a while. Think of it this way. A bull charges forward, moving ahead, like a rising market when stock prices are going up, while a bear growls or retreats like in a falling market when prices are going down."

"What are some other buzzwords?" Ruth asked.

"Oh, there are so many. I'll try to give a few, but as we go through our exercise they will pop up automatically. Equity means ownership, as do the words, stocks and shares. They are used interchangeably. Your broker may say to you , 'you are long 100 shares of ABC stock.' They only mean that you own these shares. Going short means you sold shares that you didn't own."

"Pardon," Annie said. "How can you do that?"

"You can borrow stock from your brokerage house and sell it. Let's say we borrow 1,000 shares and sell them for $7 and the price of the stock over the next week falls to $5. We would then buy the stock at $5 and return the shares to the broker and we've made $2 per share profit."

"That's interesting!" Annie said, sitting at full attention.

"This transaction is very risky and should be left only to the sophisticated trader. We know how far the stock price can fall, to zero, but we are in real trouble if the stock, after we've borrowed and sold it, goes up. We can't predict how high it'll go, and at some point the broker will want the stock returned and we may be forced to buy it back at say $12 or even higher, creating a substantial loss. It is very risky."

"I understand," Annie said, disappointed after being sure that she had found a fast way to make money.

"Why do the prices fluctuate so much during the day?" Ruth asked.

"It is really a function of market conditions. There are always two prices quoted on a stock. The bid and the ask price. The bid price is the highest price a buyer is willing to pay for a stock and the asking price is the lowest price for which a seller is willing to sell his stock. And the buyers and sellers are generally different throughout the day," Liz responded.

"I see that all the time in the real estate market," I said.

"Actually, Barb, the industries are very similar, except securities moves faster due to the liquidity in the market. But that's a great analogy. And this is where supply and demand enters the picture again. One of the problems with real estate as an investment is the lack of liquidity. The real estate market generally has more homes for sale than buyers, so it can take some time to sell a property, but the stock market, for the most part is very liquid. It certainly is on the Toronto exchange. An investor may experience a problem if they own shares in a small company listed on the Vancouver or Alberta exchange," Liz said.

"Liz, you talked about insurance protection in the trust industry and I know the banks fall into the same category, but what about insurance coverage in the securities industry?" Judy asked.

"Securities of any kind do not have insurance similar to the bank and trust company insurance offered through the Canada Deposit Insurance Corporation, which is a government program. There is, however, an organization called The Canadian Investor

Protection Fund, which will cover losses incurred due to the bankruptcy or closing of an investment firm. When you buy a stock, mutual fund or bond or even a Treasury Bill, which is issued by the government, there is no insurance. This is why the returns are higher remember the higher the return, the greater the risk. But trust me, none of us will ever get rich or even comfortable financially if we don't take some risk," Liz explained. "You have to be cautious when you are investing, know what you are buying and hold it, sometimes for a long time, because history tells us that over time, a stock investment outperforms every other investment option available."

"But Liz, what about the stock market crash in 1987? Didn't people lose a lot of money? It really scares me. I can't afford to take my hard-earned money and risk it," Annie asked, concerned.

"You know Annie, a number of investors who lost money in '87 did so because they bought at the very top of a long-term rising market. They panicked and sold just after the correction and they made a big mistake."

"I think what you are suggesting, Liz," Ruth said, "is that they should have invested more after the crash or at least hung on."

"That's right, Ruth. In hindsight the smart approach would have been to buy more to average down their costs and let their investments grow. These people will probably never go back into the market again. They are the vocal people you hear saying that market is far too risky for them and that they lost everything. Being in the market for a short term is called speculating, not investing."

"You certainly are confident that this is the proper approach," Judy said.

"You know, when I first started in this business, I, like most of us, was way behind in my personal financial situation. Most women of my generation enter the work force later in life, after the kids are grown, or after the death of a spouse or divorce. I had all those missed years to make up and I realized that if I didn't invest in the market, I would never be able to retire early, let alone in the style that I felt I deserved. If I had just put my money in the bank I would have had to continue working until I was 65 or even longer. If I was going to have to work another 25 years anyway, there really was no risk, because I knew what the down side was. What I didn't know was the upside. So for me there was no alternative, the risk was worth it. If I was going to have to stay in the work force anyway, I had nothing to lose, but if I changed my investment approach, I at least had a chance to change my lifestyle, and my plan worked. I not only took a chance with my investments, I took a career chance. My net worth is three times what it was 10 years ago. There is no question that if I had panicked in October 1987 and sold my holdings, I would not be in the position that I am today, but I never wavered. After the market crashed, I doubled my monthly investment and, as my income grew each year and every time the market dropped in value, I added to my portfolio. I am where I am today because of that strategy."

"I don't know. I guess it is because this is such a new approach. It'll take time to think about my savings differently," Annie said.

"You are at a different point in time than the rest of us, Annie. I think security is the top priority for women with small children," Ruth stated. "The children are the priority and their well-being is the most important factor and that is as it should be."

"But you don't have to take great risks, Annie," Liz suggested.

"It is so important that you and Mark start planning for the future today. The earlier in life you begin, the longer you have to build a financial wall around you. If you wait until you are my age, you'll have to put away 10 times the amount of money that you'll have to put away if you start now.

"Do you know that if you set aside $100 or even $50 a month starting now you'll be in a better financial position at age 60 than most, because you've got time working in your favour? The longer you have, the less you have to invest. I wish somebody had explained this to me when I was your age or even younger, but unfortunately, our priorities are different at different times in our life.

"If you had begun putting $50 a month into an investment fund that averaged 12 percent, compounded annually for Brett when he was born, and you and he continued the $50 investment until he was 65, he would have over eight million dollars."

Everyone gasped.

"I know that sounds impossible, but that's what the magic of compounding does for an investment."

"What do you mean by compounding?" Annie asked.

"That's when your investment income earns income for you. If the $50 a month investment for Brett earns 12 percent or $72 a year and that $72 is reinvested and earns its own 12 percent next year, it is called compounding, and it is the most powerful investment tool available."

"I read something very interesting last night," Ruth declared. "It was an article on financial planning and it explained the power of compounding. It explained the Rule of 72, a way to establish what rate of return you need to get in order to double your investment."

"Yes Ruth, the Rule of 72 is a quick calculation which is used in the industry all the time," Liz said.

"How does it work, Ruth?" Cathy asked.

"Correct me if I'm wrong, Liz, but if you divide the rate of return into the number 72, that'll tell you how many years it'll take to double your money," Ruth stated.

"That's right, Ruth," Liz said. "If you are currently averaging 10 percent on your investments, 10 into 72 says that your money will double every 7.2 years."

"Can you reinvest the income in a stock?" Judy questioned.

"Yes, some stocks offer a dividend reinvestment program, but I was referring to a mutual fund, which is another lesson."

"Look at the time," Annie said. "Brett will be starving again. I can't believe how absorbed we get listening to you Liz. The time just flies."

"This is wonderful. I've learned so much today that I can't wait until next month," Ruth said.

"Take your packages from the stock exchange, go over the information and list your questions. Everything we learned today and more is contained in the packages that Barb obtained for us. Did anybody receive their Canada Pension Plan statement yet?"

Liz asked.

"They told me it would be at least a month," Judy replied. "I can't believe that it takes so long."

"Don't forget to read the papers and watch a money show on TV, and we'll see you next month," Liz concluded as we began scurrying down the walk.

"Bundle up, cover your ears, make sure your coat is done up," Ruth called from the doorway.

We all laughed as we headed to the warmth of our homes.

Ruth, our surrogate mother.

Chapter Four
December

It surprised me, with Christmas just a few weeks away, that everyone was still anxious to meet. I only have a small family and just a few gifts to buy, but even I felt the pressure of the upcoming season. Yet each one of them arrived at my house, eager to continue the sessions.

Ruth had previously suggested that we draw names so we could exchange small gifts, tokens of our new-found friendships. Everyone settled around the Christmas tree and we chuckled when we looked at the presents and realized that they were all the same shape.

Books.

After we opened them, we placed them side by side on the table, and it was then that we realized each one was different, yet almost the same. They were all financial books.

"At least we are all on the right track. We have the start of our own little library," Ruth pointed out.

"Yes, let's exchange them throughout the year. And here I thought that I was being so unique," Cathy said.

$$$$ **75** $$$$

"I guess that we had better start the meeting before we get into a Christmas spirit and forget what we are trying to do," Liz suggested.

"Liz, I have a question," Annie began. "I've been watching the financial report on the TV news every night, and they report whether the TSE index is up or down and what the price of gold did during the day, as well as the dollar. They always quote the Dow Jones Industrial Average as well. Will you explain that to me?"

"I am so pleased that you are watching the business report, Annie, as it is the best way to get a sense of what this exercise is all about. Let's start with the dollar."

"Yes, I understand that one. It slips through my fingers quite easily," Annie said.

"There is a little more to it than just spending it, Annie. All world currencies are measured against the U.S. dollar," Liz explained. "So if the Canadian dollar is up, it means that it'll take fewer of our dollars to buy U.S. dollars and, if it is down, more. The English Pound, the Deutsche Mark and the Japanese Yen - all of the currencies in the world are measured against the U.S. dollar. It's an important economic indicator and the dollar is watched very closely by the government, economists, overseas investors and anyone else who can be affected by it."

"Yes, it even affects us when we travel outside the country. We went shopping last week for Christmas gifts in the U.S. We hardly bought anything because by the time we converted our money, the cost of things was greater than here," Judy said.

'That's right, but a visitor to Canada from the U.S. this year is finding it relatively inexpensive, at least a better bargain than years past," Liz stated. "So tourism can be affected dramatically by the rise or fall of currency. It also affects trading with other countries, and it can influence the stock market, as well. If a company has international interests - let's say that they are building a factory in another country - they must convert their Canadian dollars into a foreign currency to pay the tradesmen and buy materials. The currency rate can have a substantial effect on their bottom line. If an individual investor has money invested in another country, he or she will watch the currencies closely."

"That makes sense," Annie said, nodding her head.

"What about gold? It must be a popular investment. As you can see, I purchase my fair share," I said, flashing my jewellery.

"Gold is one of my favourite investments," Liz offered. "It is used as a hedge or protection against inflation. If it is viewed that inflation is about to rear its ugly head, the price of gold will go up. It is also a safe haven in politically troubled times and is hoarded by many people all over the world. Gold is very important and is a critical measurement of economic and political conditions, as well as having an industrial use in the form of jewellery. You are a testament to that, Barb."

"Well, I am worth it, you know!" I stated defensively.

"So are a lot of other people, which can increase the demand for jewellery and ultimately its price."

"How can you invest in gold, other than Barb's way," Annie asked Liz, as she jiggled her wrist to imitate me.

"You can buy gold bars, coins, certificates, shares in a gold mining company, or futures or options, which is a sophisticated strategy to lock in today's prices. You can even invest in gold through a mutual fund."

"I didn't realize that gold had such an important role in the world scheme of things," Ruth said surprised. "No wonder the price is quoted every day in the news."

"That's right, and the price you hear quoted on the TV and see in the paper is usually in U.S. dollars."

"Is it a good investment?" Ruth inquired.

"Ruth, the questions you ask lead me to believe that there is a risk-taker being cultivated here," Liz responded.

"Maybe! Is it a good investment?" she pushed.

"Everything is a good investment if you buy it at the right time. Timing is most important. You can wait a long time for gold to rise in price, but if you owned gold in the late seventies and early eighties and sold it when it hit $800 an ounce, you would have made a lot of money. There are followers of gold who say the time is right to buy it now, but some of these people have been saying that for years, and are still waiting."

"Do you own any gold investments, Liz?" I asked.

"Yes, and I follow the gold market. Of course, I missed the big movement in the early '80s, but I think gold should only form part of a large portfolio."

"Do you think we should invest in gold?" Ruth asked.

"The gold market is extremely risky and certainly not advisable for first-time investors, like you. The prices fluctuate daily, and an investor can wait a long time for a good price movement. Chances are you'll be disappointed. I own gold through a mutual fund and through shares in a large gold-producing company. The problem with gold is that while you are waiting for the price to rise, you receive no income, unless you buy shares in a gold-producing company and it pays a dividend to its shareholders.

"Speculators can make big money when they find a mining company that is still in the exploration stage and then the company discovers gold. In the beginning, during the early stages of exploration, the shares are priced very low, but if they strike gold, the stock price will rise rapidly. The reality is, you may buy shares in a number of different companies before you find one that actually finds gold. You must be careful when you buy shares in a company that is in the exploration stage - there is no guarantee that they will discover gold. It is at this stage, when they need the money the most, that many promotions take place to raise the capital to help with their costs. A lot of investors get caught up in the story, rather than the fundamentals of the company."

"Have you ever made money in gold, Liz?" Ruth asked.

"Yes, the first time I invested in the stock market was in a gold mining company. I received information from a friend when I first started in the business, before I was licensed, and I invested $3,000, with which I bought shares at around $3. The stock rose to $9 and I sold my shares. I bought it back at $12 and sold at $18, bought it again at $21 and sold it again at $27."

"Wow!" Annie exclaimed.

"Yes, it was great, and that's probably why I am a bit of a gold bug, but then I bought stock in another mining venture in 1985, sure that it would generate the same results. It too, had a great story, it was right next door to a major producer and they felt that the strike ran on to their property. I bought shares anywhere from 75¢ to $2 and bought quite a number. Today the shares have been as low as 6¢, although they are starting to rise again because the promoters have raised more money from the public. This money will enable them to return to the property and continue their search for the gold. I can only hope that this time I'll get my money out before it's gone again. Any other questions about gold?"

"Yes, I have," Annie said. "We found what appears to be a coin collection among my Dad's things. We didn't think much about it at the time, but do you think we should have someone look at it? I know there are gold coins in there."

"Definitely. Depending on what he has, and how old the coins are, they could be very valuable. Coin dealing is a big business," Liz replied.

"Okay, we have covered the dollar and gold. Let's go on to the indexes," Liz suggested. "The stock exchanges report by index, and I'll explain what that means in a minute, but first you must understand that the TSE listings are broken down into different categories called sectors: Minerals, Golds, Oil and Gas, Forestry, Consumer Products, Industry, Pipelines, Utilities, Communications, Merchandise, Financial, Management, Building, Transportation and Biotech. These sectors can, and often do, move in different directions at different times during a day or a business cycle. This is a result of the perception of what is happening in the economy. By following the movement of individual sectors, economists and investment advisors try to anticipate what the markets will do. They then counsel their clients accordingly.

"Each one of these sectors has an index. An index is basically a barometer which measures the specific industry's share price movement," Liz explained.

"Which index should we be paying attention to?" Ruth questioned.

"The TSE 300. It reflects the price of 300 common stocks and is the most commonly referred to index in Canada, though each exchange has its own index . When you hear on the news that the TSE 300 index rose 10 points today, and if you are invested in the companies included in the index, chances are your stocks are up in price. This is not a guarantee as the index is an average and some stocks could be down."

"Is it fair to say that the TSE index is a quick reference as to how the markets are doing?" I asked.

"Yes, that is a good statement, Barb. Assuming that the prices tend to move up or down together, it indicates a direction. But you must also watch the Dow Jones Industrial Average in New York. It is the blue chip index and because the U.S. market is the largest single market in the world, it is very important to watch what it is doing."

"You mean that Canada reacts to the news in the U.S.?" I asked.

"No question about it. The movement of Canada's markets is directly related to what happens in the U.S. and it is not uncommon for our markets to react to U.S. news and more commonly, if the U.S. market is down, ours will be as well, or will be the next day. There is an old saying that if the United States sneezes, Canada catches a cold. It certainly is true when talking about the stock market."

"Liz, if the markets rise and fall, how can you protect yourself from price fluctuations?" Ruth asked.

"Well, Ruth, I can only give you the benefit of what I've learned over the past 10 years and that is that diversification is the best way to protect yourself from the price fluctuations," Liz stated.

"What do you mean?" Cathy asked.

"If you buy different stocks in many sectors or various types of investments, you are protecting yourself. If one or two of them decline in price, hopefully the rest will rise in value and offset any loss."

"But don't you have to have a lot of money in order to do this?" Annie asked.

"Usually, but you can also diversify through a mutual fund, where the manager buys many different investments or stocks. This is actually why the mutual fund industry was created. In order for small investors to obtain the diversification required to protect their money, they, along with thousands of other investors, pool their money, enabling the manager to buy many stocks, which provides the diversification," Liz explained.

"Bob has a mutual fund in one of his RRSPs," Ruth declared.

"That's a good plan, because they both have long-term horizons. They are perfect together," Liz said.

"What's a mutual fund?" Cathy asked.

"I think we should continue on with the stock market, until most of your questions are answered, before we venture into the world of mutual funds. The underlying investments in a mutual fund are primarily stocks and bonds. I want you to be well-versed on these two vehicles, so you are able to select a proper mutual fund."

"Liz, what do you do if you have bought a stock and realize that you've made a mistake?" Ruth asked.

"If you find that you have made a mistake and bought a stock that hasn't performed as you had hoped, and in all likelihood won't in the near future, the best thing to do is sell it."

"You really only have two options, right, Liz," I said, "hold it, and hope it comes back or sell it, take your loss, walk away and go on to something else. We see this with real estate speculators all the time."

"That's right, Barb. One of the worst things you can do is to become emotionally attached to a stock and hold and hold until you hate it. When you lose money on a stock, you automatically cringe when you hear its name mentioned," Liz explained.

"How can you avoid making a mistake?" Ruth questioned.

"Ruth, you'll make some mistakes, and if you don't, I'll let you manage my money. Everybody makes bad investment choices at one time or another, but you shouldn't get discouraged. Buy smart, always look for value, and don't buy a stock that you haven't thoroughly investigated with your broker. Don't buy on tips and above all, don't buy any investment over the phone from someone you don't know. Also, don't be a short-term investor. I've missed out on tremendous gains because I sold too early."

"Liz, what are some of the things we should check when we are looking to buy a stock. Any insider tips?" Annie asked.

"Good question. One of the easiest and most important items to check is the price of the stock over the past year. A broker can tell you what the high and low price was during the past 52-week period. This will tell you where the price is, in relationship to where it was, and if it is at its high, the broker should be able to justify why he or she thinks it is going to go higher. If it is at a low, you would want to know why, what made it drop, and why should it recover."

"What are some of the reasons a stock should or shouldn't recover?" Ruth asked.

"A stock price can fall due to a change in senior management or as a result of poor management. You would want to know what steps have been taken to correct the situation. A product can fail or, as we all remember a few years ago when poison was found in an over-the-counter cold pill, adverse publicity can hurt a company. A lawsuit often drags a stock price down, and any material item that can affect the bottom line should be investigated. The severity of the problem will tell you whether or not the stock should recover. Remember, you are the investor and there are millions of others like you out there. Again, use your common sense. If you are appalled or affected emotionally by a problem that a company has, other investors will be too, and this ultimately affects the stock price.

"Another thing you should check when considering a stock is whether or not it is overvalued and the way to do this is to ask the price-earnings ratio. This is an important tool used by the industry. It sounds difficult but it is quite an easy calculation, once you have the information. Here is how it works.

"The stock price is divided by the annual earnings per share. I'll give you an example. If a stock is trading at $10 and the annual earnings are $1 per share, the stock is said to be trading at 10 times earnings. You should get a figure of anywhere from five to 30 times for most Canadian stocks. Ask your broker what the average multiple is for that particular industry or sector and you can judge whether or not the stock price is in line."

"So if a stock is trading in the low range, it means that the stock is undervalued and has some room to grow. Is that right, Liz?" Ruth asked.

"It's a good indication, as long as you understand that there are exceptions and there may very well be extenuating circumstances which are affecting the stock."

"Is there any other reason people buy stock, except for the growth in the share price?" Cathy asked.

"Yes, some people buy stocks for income, dividend income. When we look at the sectors we talked about earlier, the industries that provide a steady stream of income are the utilities and financial institutions, which would include the major banks and very large trust companies, and other large-cap companies that pay a constant dividend and are generally classified as blue chip, conservative investments. Their prices fluctuate, but do so moderately," Liz explained.

"What is meant, Liz, by a large-cap company?" Annie asked.

"There are basically three sizes of listed companies: large-cap, medium-cap, and small-cap companies. First of all, capitalization means the value of the total shares issued by a company, including long-term debt or bonds issued. A large-cap company has a capitalization over $500 million. An example would be a major bank or Bell Canada, which is considered large-cap, as is Canadian Pacific. On the other hand, a small-cap company value is under $200 million, and a mid-cap somewhere in between the two."

"Do companies only issue one type of stock? I seem to remember my dad buying stock but I don't think he would risk any of his money," Cathy questioned.

"Individual companies issue shares and bonds with different features and classes of shares. It isn't necessary to know every one available, but it is important to understand why companies do it and how different types of shares can be used in an investment portfolio. The stocks that we have dealt with so far are called common stocks, but many companies issue what are called preferred shares."

"Does that mean that they are a preferred investment over common stock?" Ruth inquired.

"No, it means that a preferred shareholder will be paid before a common shareholder, hence its name. It is not necessarily a preferred investment, but it gets preferential treatment if the company goes bankrupt or winds up its affairs for whatever reason. If a company has issued bonds, preferred shares and common shares, the bondholders get paid first, the preferred shareholders second and the common shareholders last, if there is anything left. The preferred shareholders also receive a pre-determined dividend which has preferential treatment as well, and not unlike a bond, it is sensitive to interest rates. Remember when interest rates rise, bond and preferred share prices fall, and when interest rates fall, bond and preferred shares rise to adjust for the stated interest rate. Preferred shares are also rated according to quality, not unlike bonds, with the highest rating granted to the best quality preferred share. Older investors like preferred shares because of the dividend income which they generate."

"So, a preferred share is less risky than a common share, is that right, Liz?" Ruth asked.

"Generally, Ruth. However if a company is experiencing difficulties, I wouldn't buy their preferred shares either. Many a time a company has declared bankruptcy and the preferred holders ultimately find out that there isn't enough money to pay them, either. The preferred shares also come with different features attached to them."

"What type of features?" Ruth queried.

"Well, there are convertible preferred shares, which means that preferred shares can be converted into or exchanged for a specific number of common shares. Or a company may stipulate that preferred shares can be called or bought back by the corporation at a specific price. These are referred to as callable preferred share. A company may also issue a cumulative preferred share. In this case no dividends may be paid to common shareholders if preferred stock dividends are in arrears. Actually most preferred stocks are cumulative."

"Please explain the dividends," Cathy said. "Where does the company get the money to pay the dividends?"

"Dividends represent a portion of the company's net earnings after tax. Preferred shares generally pay dividend income. Common shares do not necessarily generate a dividend. It is really up to the directors of a company. They may decide that all income earned during the year is to be used for the continued growth of the company and use the money to expand or invest in new equipment or another enterprise."

"What happens to the stock when a company pays a dividend? Does the price of the shares go up, because people want to receive the dividend?" Ruth questioned.

"It is important to understand how dividends work. Some investors look for dividend-generating stocks and buy and sell them around the dividend date, depending on their tax situation. If you buy a stock around the time a dividend is to be paid by the company, you'll either be ex-dividend, not entitled to it, or cum-dividend, entitled to it. You must be a shareholder on what is called the record date, which can be up to a month before the dividend is paid. If you sell the share the day after the record date, you'll still get the dividend and the purchaser will be ex-dividend. It is possible that the share price will rise before the record date and be a bit lower days after."

"I have a question, Liz, what are rights and warrants?" Cathy asked.

"I can tell by your questions that you guys did your homework and read the information from the stock exchanges. Good students," she laughed.

"A right is the privilege given to a shareholder by a company to acquire additional shares directly from the company. The number of shares offered is in direct relationship to the number of shares you currently hold. The company may say you have the right to buy one additional share for each two shares that you currently own and specify a time frame, which is fairly short, in which you may do this. The price is generally lower than the then current market price. A warrant is different. It gives the holder of the warrant the option of buying a specific number of shares at a set price until a certain date. Warrants will expire worthless if the stock never reaches the offering price. Rights and warrants trade in the market place like stocks but ultimately disappear after the specified time has elapsed," Liz explained.

"You mean, if a warrant entitles you to purchase additional stock at $5 and the stock never reaches $5 before the warrant expires, you wouldn't exercise your privilege to buy it."

"No, why would you? Your warrant simply is of no value and it expires."

"Liz," Ruth said, stopping for a moment from her furious note taking. "Speaking about prices, when you want to buy a stock, do you state a price that you want to pay for it?"

"Good question Ruth. When buying and selling stock, you have to be specific and cautious with your instructions. If you say that you want to buy a particular stock at $5, you have then placed a limit order and the broker will not buy the stock unless he can obtain it for $5. If a stock is at $5.25 and continues on a upward price movement, you won't own it until it comes back to $5, if it ever does. If you want to own the stock, instruct the broker to buy it 'at market.' The broker will then buy the stock for you at the best price available. The same thing applies when you are selling a stock. However, unless you are desperate or there is an urgency to sell, you can state a specific selling price, especially if you have a benchmark for your profit. If a stock I own has performed well and I am happy with my profit or if I am going to be away, I'll put in an open order to sell only when the stock hits a certain price. Be very specific when making your request and ensure that the broker understands what the instructions are. I've lost out on a number of good investments for my clients when they have been less than clear about exactly what they wanted to do."

"Liz, when you buy a stock, do you get a certificate like a Canada Savings Bond or a GIC?" I asked.

"You can. But I don't advise it. Many a certificate is lost this way. All listed companies use a transfer agent, usually a trust company, to record all the names and addresses of the shareholders and the number of shares they own. If you would like a certificate, you can ask the broker to register the shares in your name and deliver the certificate to your home. It is much easier, and a more common practice, however, to let the broker keep the shares in their company name. This is called 'street form' or the shares are said to be in 'street name.' The number of shares owned will show in your account and every month you'll receive a statement showing any transactions and the number and value of the shares held. This eliminates the need for you to put them in a safety deposit box or to have to worry about the dividends or any pertinent action that must be taken concerning the stock. If you neglect to notify the transfer agent of a change of address, you won't receive any information. It is much better to let the broker take care of the details."

"Boy, am I ever glad that we had time to go over all the information that Barb got us from the stock exchanges before we had this session, because you have clarified a lot of points," Cathy said. "I've been so engrossed I've eaten all the Christmas sandwiches."

"Besides individuals, who else buys stock?" I asked as I picked up the tray to refill it.

"Actually 80 percent of all publicly traded equity investments are held by institutions. You'll be pleased to know that if you buy a stock you are in great company, as one of the reasons the market does so well over time and the volume of shares traded every day is so high is the buying and selling done by major institutions," Liz explained.

"If you have a pension plan at work, its manager buys stock for your plan. Insurance companies and banks also buy stock. Money managers who invest on behalf of millions of mutual fund clients are buying stock in large blocks as well. If money managers have a lot of cash, and the time is right, they will buy a large number of shares. They do so in any company that they decide will grow and produce a good return for their investors, provided the money managers stay within the guidelines set out in the prospectus which is the document that guides the investment strategy of the fund. Foreigners also purchase Canadian stock. They may want to diversify their investments outside their own country. Canada has historically been viewed as one of the most politically stable countries in the world and our natural resources are of great interest to outsiders. For example, if the price of gold is on the rise, demand picks up, and companies that produce gold will be of interest to the rest of the world. Canada is one of the world's largest producers of gold. Lumber is another one of our great resources and it is exported to countries all over the world. If there is to be a major building boom, lumber companies will do very well. We are also one of the major suppliers of other forest products to the world, such as pulp and paper. Canada is also a major producer of oil and gas, and if the Middle East upsets the oil cart, prices increase, benefiting our oil and gas industry."

"Speaking about foreign investors, can we buy stock in foreign countries?" Judy asked.

"Yes, but it can be difficult, with the exception of the United States, which is easily available through major Canadian brokerage houses. If you buy stock in a foreign country, you are considered a non-resident and just as we do with foreign investors in Canada, you are subject to a withholding tax on income received from foreign sources. In the U.S. the withholding tax for Canadian investors is 15 percent."

"You mean if you earn $100 in income they withhold $15?" Cathy asked. "Isn't that a form of double taxation?"

"No, when you complete your income tax return you include the $15 as tax already paid and you are allowed a tax credit, which ensures that you don't pay tax twice."

"It is relatively easy to buy U.S. stocks, but more difficult if you want to buy in other countries, unless they have a large exchange like London, England. You can, however, buy stock through an ADR which is an American Depository Receipt. ADRs are used to simplify the trading of foreign stocks in the U.S. An ADR represents ownership in foreign securities but the shares are actually held in U.S. banks around the world. The ADR will represent the shares of the stock you want to buy. Now, not all stocks listed on world exchanges are represented through ADR, but there are quite a few and more all the time.

"I'll give you an example. I just bought an ADR which represents shares in a South American telephone company. Each ADR represents four shares and I paid, in U.S. dollars, four times the trading price of one share. This country has a very fast moving economy currently, and it makes sense that they are going to need a major telephone system, which should generate substantial profits for the investors."

"I would think that all of those countries, Mexico and other countries like Brazil, are in the same situation," Cathy stated.

"Yes, we don't realize how fortunate we are in North America to have such a sophisticated telephone system. When I visited Greece a few years ago it was almost impossible to call home," Liz recalled. "I had to line up at a bank phone, which is the only public phone available, for hours and after being connected for only a few minutes, I was cut off."

"Other than the ADR, are there other ways to invest in foreign countries? On TV last week they referred to a country fund," Ruth mentioned.

"Yes, these are generally closed-end mutual funds which invest in specific countries such as China, Korea, India or the South American countries, where it is difficult or cumbersome for an individual to acquire shares."

"There it is again - mutual funds," Cathy said. "Are you going to explain them now?"

"Well, I'll explain closed-end funds, because they operate more like a stock than a mutual fund and we'll leave the other type until January. A closed-end fund is not unlike a stock except that you are not investing in an operating company, but in a corporation that has been set up to manage money in a specific type of investment or area. There are closed-end real estate funds, income funds, gold funds and country funds. The company that offers the fund to the public, generally a money manager or broker, will offer shares at a specific price for a period of time."

"How long Liz?" asked Barb.

"Oh, 45, to say, 90 days. They then close the investment to the public and no additional shares are issued. If the shares are sold at $10 and 10,000,000 shares are issued, the company receives $100 million, less commission, from investors. Remember, just like a new stock issue, the corporation, not the public, pays the commission. The shares are listed on a stock exchange and the manager of the fund invests the money, say in South American countries. Over a period of time, the manager buys stocks in this market and while he is doing this, the shares in the closed-end fund trade on the open market."

"What if another investor wants to buy shares? " asked Ruth.

"If an investor, after the fund has closed, wants to buy shares of the fund, he does so through a stock broker and buys them in the open market like a stock, for whatever price the market has established. This market price can be higher or lower than the initial $10 book value that the original investors paid. If it is trading lower than $10 it is said to be trading at a discount to net asset value or NAV, and if it is trading higher, at a premium. It is a pretty good concept, because no matter what the market demands, the manager is never in a position where he is forced to sell the underlying investments. If there is a rush to sell from the public, they must sell their shares in the open market. So there are two prices when you are dealing with a closed-end fund: the market price, which the public sets through supply and demand, and the asset value, which truly reflects the value of the investments."

"Liz, we have certainly learned a lot today," Ruth said. "I can't wait to watch my financial show on Saturday. I wondered why they gave us the figures on the Japanese market. Now I know. It seems to me that the world has just become smaller and that what happens elsewhere can affect us dramatically."

"That's right, Ruth, Canada only represents three percent of the world stock markets, which together are valued today at around nine trillion dollars. It's like the elephant and the mouse story, Canada being the mouse. There is very little that we can do to affect the elephant. I really believe that in order to get the most out of your investments you have to invest outside of Canada with at least some of your money. And the Japanese market is as important to the American market as that market is to Canada.

"At one point in time a few years ago, the Japanese market outgrew the U.S. market and I think that really surprised the Americans. It has since changed, but the Japanese market is still a close second. There are so many opportunities to earn a good return in faster-growing and emerging economies. It is important that we don't overlook them. With today's communications and sophisticated computer programs available, there is no reason not to participate abroad.

"You can also take part by investing through Canadian companies which are focusing on the international marketplace. I have an investment in a Canadian oil company that is drilling for oil in Indonesia, and there are many others. Many companies will be involved in the growth of the Russian market when they get things straightened out over there. It may take a while, but the potential is there, as well as in Eastern Europe. The vast amounts of investment dollars that it'll take to bring that area up to western prosperity standards is enormous, but you can be certain that there will be North American companies participating in that growth, and all we, as investors, have to do is to identify which ones they are and grow with them. This is why, for the individual, it is so important to read and keep up with world events. Also, it is key to work with a financial advisor who understands the world markets.

"One of the risks you take when buying outside of Canada is currency fluctuation. If you buy a foreign investment and the Canadian dollar rises, you could have a loss because you are invested in a foreign currency. If the Canadian dollar falls, you would not only participate in the growth of the investment, but when you convert your money back to Canadian, you'll buy cheaper dollars, so you'll gain on the currency exchange as well. This is one added consideration when you are investing in a foreign country."

"There is a lot to think about, isn't there, Liz?" Ruth said. "Just trying to decide which investment, which company, what sector of the market, what country - it is almost overwhelming."

"That's why there are professional investment managers available. I never said that you should do your own investing - I only wanted you to have an understanding of how the markets work, in order for us to go on to the next step.

"Until you are fairly sophisticated in the markets, I highly recommend hiring a professional money manager, with the assistance of a financial advisor. But we'll get into this next month. I feel that you are ready to go on. In the meantime, I gathered information from some of the top investment managers and have separate stacks for you. Even though it is Christmas, you should be able to read a bit and get a feel for this part of the industry before the next meeting."

"Can anybody get this information, as we did from the stock exchanges?" I asked.

"Yes, the managers provide a toll-free telephone number and most will send the information to you. You may also contact any stockbroker or independent financial advisor or your bank and they'll send you this same information. Money managers spend millions of dollars educating the public through their materials, which are very easy to read because they are aimed directly at the consumer. You can also telephone The Investment Funds Institute of Canada, an association that most of the firms belong to, and they'll send you valuable information."

"This is wonderful, I feel so in control," Ruth said.

"Better go. It's Brett's dinner time again," Annie said.

"It's amazing - that, child must eat three times a day!" Judy laughed.

"Oh look! It's snowing," Ruth said peering out through the drapes.

"Merry Christmas and Happy New Year, everyone. See you next year at Cathy's house," I said.

"Happy reading," Liz commented

Chapter Five
January

Cathy's house smelled of home baked cookies and fresh flowers.

"Whatever have you been baking Cathy? It's making me hungry," Annie asked.

"Actually I haven't baked anything, it's Cal, he made us brownies."

"This has to be the coldest winter in Canada's history," Ruth complained as she came through the door yanking her boots off. "I've never seen so much snow. I need a vacation in the south, now. Oh my, what smells so good?"

She was the last one to arrive.

"Cal's baking brownies and don't we all need a vacation!" Annie said. "Wouldn't it be nice if we could continue the rest of our sessions in the Bahamas?"

"Yes, we could call it a foreign educational trip," I piped in.

"Well, I can't afford it," Judy stammered. "I have to work double time to ensure that I don't starve to death when I retire. I received my Canada Pension Plan statement two weeks ago."

"Oh good, Judy, let's take a look at it," Liz said.

"Oh good?" stammered Judy. "I am in a rage. I want to know how this happens. I ordered Paul's statement as well. You know, we worked for the same company at one time. Actually, that's where we met and then he changed jobs. Anyway, here we were working for the same company and doing the same job. I knew that he was paid more than I was, but I didn't realize the long-term ramifications. According to our statements, Paul will receive a full Canada Pension and I'll get 40 percent less. I'm furious at him, the company, the government, the whole system."

"This is why I wanted you to get your statements," Liz pointed out. "The critical factor which affects women is that unless you earn a specific amount each year which allows you to contribute the maximum amount to the Canada Pension Plan, you'll not receive a full pension at age 65. They do make an adjustment for interrupted working years due to the raising of children, but this doesn't change the fundamental problem. Women who step out of the work force to have children can interrupt what may be a promising career and it takes years to recover from those lost earnings. Some women never recover."

"So, what you are saying is, as long as you are not earning a certain wage, you are not able to contribute enough to provide a full pension," Judy continued.

"Yes, and if, as is predicted by many, the Old Age Pension is not available at some point in the future, women are in serious trouble," Liz replied.

"Let me get this straight, Liz. Unless, when our husbands are planning to retire, we refuse to sign the waiver, we'll not be entitled to any of his company pension. Also, it is entirely possible that most of us will not get a full Canada Pension, unless we earn a certain salary throughout our careers. And now you are saying that there is a possibility that the government will stop the Old Age Pension. Unless we have our own pensions, we are all going to be on welfare," Annie protested.

"That's a real possibility," Liz stated.

"But Liz, I should be fine," Cathy stated. "I have my teacher's pension, and other women who have private pension plans will be all right."

"Certainly they will. However the lower earnings will be a factor with private plans as well. The problem today is that pension rules have become so complicated and have made the defined-benefit plan like yours, Cathy, so expensive to administer that many corporations are exploring the possibility of unwinding them. Companies that don't currently offer them are reluctant to put them in place for their employees for these very reasons.

"In addition, a defined-benefit plan provides a pension based on earnings and the number of years an employee and the employer have contributed to the plan. The legislation does allow portability, meaning the ability to transfer from one employer's pension plan to another. However, in practice there are very few private pension plans that will accept your pension money into their plan. The exception would be a government sector plan like yours, Cathy. It is my understanding that teacher's pension plans have reciprocal agreements. In the private sector, in order to have a full pension, an individual must continue working for the same company and contribute, for years, to the same plan," Liz explained.

"What you are saying is that, unless you work for the same employer for about 30 years, you won't have a full pension," Ruth said. "But very few people today stay with the same employer for the lifetime of their career."

"That's right, and in addition to that, if a spouse is designated to receive the company pension, it'll only entitle them to approximately 60 percent of the initial pension payment after death, this information says," Judy said pointing to a booklet on her pension from her company.

"But that doesn't make sense. My taxes wouldn't drop by 40 percent, nor would my heating bills or my car payment. The only savings would be in food or dry cleaning and things like that. In fact, if I wanted to take a vacation alone, it would cost more to travel as a single," Ruth exclaimed.

"I know. I didn't say that what happens is proper, only that it happens," Judy said.

"What makes you think that they will stop the Old Age Pension, Liz?" Ruth asked.

"For the next 40 or 50 years there are going to be fewer people in the work force to support a growing number of retired workers. This will place a tremendous burden on the government's available resources, and a number of analysts and political figures have predicted that the Old Age Pension will have to go. I think that the first thing they will do is create a means test or a needs test," Liz explained.

"You mean, instead of giving a supplement for low income earners as they do today, they'll say, if you are earning a certain amount of income you'll receive no pension?" Cathy asked.

"Yes, but I think that they'll not just look at income generated from your investments, they'll also look at your net worth, as they do with the welfare program," Liz stated. "I believe this is why the RRSP rules are so liberal today. The government knows that the day of reckoning is coming and that some people will only have their RRSPs to live on."

"Why don't they tell the public that this is what will happen in the future, so we can prepare?" Annie asked.

"I think that they'll leave it until the day it happens. No political party wants to be in power and take the wrath of the public when something this drastic affects so many voters."

"Wow, this is scary stuff," Annie said, shaking her head. "What is the solution?"

"We must start taking control of our future. This is the reason that we've been learning about investments, right?" Liz said.

"Right!" We all cheered.

"Alright, let's get going. We have a lot to absorb today," Liz prompted.

"Yes, let's continue," Annie said. "You have scared me."

"Sorry about that, but I really believe that we are going to be in serious trouble if we don't start planning today."

"Okay, okay, let's start. Teach us fast," Annie prompted whirling her hand.

"Last month we talked briefly about using diversification as a protection against risk. One of the best investment vehicles available to accomplish this is an open-ended mutual fund."

"Now I can ask. What is a mutual fund?" Cathy was anxious to finally receive an answer to her persistent question.

"A mutual fund is a corporation or a trust that holds a portfolio of securities but is actually owned by individual shareholders. All of the shareholders receive the same rate of return, and participate in the growth and income generated by the securities or other investments within the fund," Liz explained.

"What is the difference between an open-ended fund and a closed-end fund, Liz?" Cathy asked.

"The open-ended fund continuously issues shares and the fund buys your shares back if you want to sell. Remember, the closed-end fund issues a specific number of shares which trade in the open market."

"Doesn't it become expensive for the fund to buy back the shares?" Annie asked.

"No, the mutual fund is owned by the shareholders and if you want to sell your units, you are really getting back your own money."

"What if the manager or the fund, rather, doesn't have the cash?" she continued with her questions.

"The manager will simply sell some of the underlying investments, the stocks or bonds. But all managers keep enough cash in reserve to meet the normal requests of redeeming shareholders."

"What are the mechanics of a redemption, Liz?" Annie asked.

"The fund is valued at the end of each day by adding up the closing day's prices of all of the investments, deducting the liabilities, then dividing the balance by the total number of units that the shareholders own, to arrive at a unit price. The manager then sends you a cheque for your share. You don't have to worry, you'll receive your money," Liz explained.

"Why haven't we been exposed to professional money managers before. Did our parents use them?" Cathy asked.

"Years ago, professional money managers were only available to the extremely wealthy. But today, everyone has access to not only Canada's, but the world's top money managers."

"I looked in the paper the other day and there was a whole list of mutual funds," Ruth commented.

"That's right. The choices are so numerous that before making a decision you could spend days trying to make a selection. Almost every financial institution offers investment funds. I think that when you are going to invest, you want a manager to be striving for the best possible return commensurate with risk. The manager is usually compensated directly by the firm for an above-average performance in two ways. First, if they are the best or at least in the list of top performers, they'll earn a bonus from their company, and second, when a manager outperforms the competition, the public rewards them by investing with them. This makes the company more profitable and some of the managers have ownership in the management company. This incentive keeps them very motivated and extremely competitive."

"How does the fund earn it's money?" Annie asked.

"The mutual fund charges a management fee annually, which varies according to the type of investment fund being managed. In addition to the management fee, the fund will incur certain expenses. In order to establish the total fee being levied against the fund by the manager, you should check the managers expense ratio, which will include all of the charges.

"The lowest expense ratio charged is generally on a money market fund, which may be anywhere from one-half to one-and-a-half percent. Bond and a mortgage funds will charge from one-half to two-and-a half percent or greater, and an equity fund's expense ratio will range from one percent to approximately three percent."

"So if a manager is good, more people invest and the manager benefits again by making more money," Ruth said, nodding her head.

"If they work hard for their money and if they are making me a lot of money, pay them a big bonus, I say," Annie stated, raising her thumb in the air.

"That's right. They do work hard. Their entire day is spent overseeing the investments that they have bought for their clients. They are committed to doing the best job possible, providing their investors with the highest rate of return, be it income or capital appreciation," Liz said.

"How do they keep up with all the information on all of the companies available?" Ruth asked.

"They have every tool of the trade available to them, including computer modules which measure different indexes, trends and programs, and they are tapped into the world news through electronic communication systems set up right on their premises. By the time you and I hear of a major event on the news at 6 p.m., they have already heard it and reacted.

"Most money managers actually visit the companies that they invest in, and they follow the company's operation to ensure that the reason they bought the stock or bond in the first place is still valid."

"You mean they actually go to the site and look at the company's operation?" Annie asked.

"You bet. A professional manager told us about a company that he visited over the years. He had been a buyer of this particular company's stock for many years and he spoke to the president often. One summer he telephoned four or five times, early in the morning and was unable to reach him, so he jumped in his car and drove to the plant. He discovered that the president had taken up golf, instead of running the business. Through his investigation he determined that the president was on the golf course three or four times a week. The manager sold his holdings in the company and rightly so, as the stock price soon started to fall. The president wasn't taking care of business."

"Good for him," Annie said, agreeing with the approach.

"The professional money manager is well versed on the market, the economy, interest rates and all of the other factors that affect stock and bond prices. Different managers don't always agree on which way the market is going to go. All the prospective purchaser can do is to look at their past performance. If their five- and 10 - year investment performance is good, it is a pretty safe bet that you have selected a seasoned professional manager. You have to rely on your financial advisor to keep you informed. These people are constantly updated by the fund managers about market conditions and what new investments are available. The money managers and their marketing department representatives travel across Canada three or four times a year, holding information meetings which financial advisors are invited to attend. These sessions inform the industry of new products and provide an update on and overview of companies or countries that they are currently investing in and strategies that they have in place to provide you, the client, with the best advice available."

"With so many different funds and manager available to the public, the competition must be fierce, Liz," Ruth said.

"No question about it, Ruth. Their performance is constantly measured and reported by all of the newspapers and industry watchers. Sellers of their products want to bring the best of the lot to their clients, so good performance is critical. They watch each other as well. One manager always wants to outperform the other. This is one of the main reasons why mutual funds are good investments. To be reported in the newspaper as having the best performing funds in the industry is the cherry on the top of the sundae."

"I would think so," Ruth said. "To have a manager trying to outperform every other manager in the industry is about the best situation an investor can be in."

"I'm starting to understand why you wanted us to have an understanding of the stock market first, Liz," Judy said.

"Good. I don't think that anyone should be investing unless they have a basic understanding of how the markets work. Some investors are surprised and devastated when the market suddenly drops. They have no idea that the markets can go down as well as up. The market never moves in a straight line and if you are buying an equity mutual fund, the underlying investment will be listed stocks, which means that if the stock market falls, your mutual fund will fall, and the same thing with bonds.

"Everything we talked about when we were learning about the stock market will fall into place shortly. Buying one or two stocks is quite different from buying a mutual fund. If you buy one stock and it falls, you have lost money, on paper at least, but when the fund manager buys 50 or a 100 different stocks and one or two drop in value, your mutual fund will hardly even feel it. So when you are buying an investment fund, your risk is reduced.

"One of the biggest mistakes that people make when investing in funds is selling at the wrong time. And investors have been doing this since the beginning of time," Liz explained.

"How can we avoid selling at the wrong time?" Ruth asked.

"First, and I don't know how to say this more clearly, if you need your money within two to three years, stay away from the stock market. This rule applies to stocks as well as mutual funds, because as sure as God made little green apples, you'll need your money at the wrong time. The markets go up and down and like interest rates, there is nothing you and I can do about it, except take advantage of it or ride it out.

"Second rule, don't panic. The market will fluctuate. That is a sure thing. Years ago, the market moved gradually. Today, the market has become volatile. Accept this as a normal function of the market and you'll be alright. Rejoice in the up days, and know that if an investment drops 10 or 15¢ in one day, it also has the ability to rise that much the next or the day after. Stay calm," Liz encouraged. "And be a long term investor."

"Not only are there a lot of mutual funds available, but the paper seems to group them into different categories, Liz," Ruth offered.

"Basically, mutual funds fall into three categories: equity, bond and money market. And from these three basic groups, the funds create their strategy. Some funds focus solely on growth and some provide growth and income. Some only provide income.

"Equity funds invest mainly in the common stock of listed companies on the different stock exchanges but they may contain a small portion of bonds as well. They come with different descriptions, such as growth, opportunities, pooled equity, enterprise, diversified, accumulating or just plain common stock fund, just to name a few. The majority of the funds available are equity funds. The goal of all equity funds is to participate in the growth of the companies they've chosen to invest in, always with an eye to preserving your invested capital. Some equity funds only invest in large-cap, blue chip companies like the major banks, Bell Canada, Interprovincial Pipe Line, Northern Telecom and so on. Others may invest in mid-size companies or small-cap or a combination of them all. The funds that invest in small-cap companies may have greater growth potential, but because some of these companies are less known or new, the risk will be greater. However, on the other side of the coin, the rewards can be greater as well, but this type of fund is generally riskier than the blue chip invested funds."

"How do you know what type of investment the manager is making, Liz?" Cathy asked.

"Every mutual fund available has what is called a prospectus. This document, generally a little booklet, explains what type of investments the manager is investing in, and before you buy any mutual fund, *read the prospectus* to know what you are buying."

"Does the manager send you the prospectus or how do you get it?" Cathy asked.

"The manager may send it to you, but that would be after you buy the fund. Ask whoever you are talking to, either your bank, trust company, insurance agent, broker or independent advisor, for the prospectus before you buy, to ensure that you understand what the fund manager's investment philosophy is and into what type of investment your hard-earned money is being placed."

"Do they invest all over the world, Liz?" Annie asked.

"An equity fund may invest outside of Canada and some funds can be purchased in either Canadian or U.S. funds. The funds that invest outside of our borders are referred to as U.S. equity or international equity funds," Liz explained.

"Does the manager travel to the different countries?" Cathy asked.

"Sometimes, but unless a Canadian manager has expertise in a specific foreign country, they'll hire an outside manager, physically located in that country, or at least, if they employ a Canadian, that person will have vast knowledge of and insight into the country. Again, these international funds may invest in well-established companies or smaller lesser-known companies. And the countries themselves can be well established, such as Japan, England, Germany and the United States, or they can be what is referred to as emerging countries, such as Argentina, Indonesia, Brazil or Mexico."

"It seems to me that if a fund is investing in a foreign country, I would look for a management company that has a manager permanently located in that country. Is that a valid concern, Liz?" Judy asked.

"Yes, I think it is. The securities and accounting rules differ from country to country and a manager must be completely knowledgeable about these rules as well as about the culture. If I had a choice between a foreign fund that was managed locally and one that was managed from Canada, I would chose the one with the manager located within the foreign country," Liz said.

"Are foreign funds riskier than Canadian ones?" Ruth asked.

"Again the risk is directly related to the development of the country, and to the political and economic environment, which the fund manager should be in tune with. An investment in the United States is almost certainly less risky than one in Argentina. However, the growth potential of a fund in a developing country can be substantial, provided the conditions are right and, again, the fund manager carefully selects and knows the country in which they invest. You can even buy a fund that may invest in any country it chooses, a world fund, which is the ultimate exposure."

"I guess for some of us, it is difficult to get a handle on what is happening in different parts of the world. We are so caught up in our day to day lives that unless you spend your full time investigating, reading and watching TV, you really develop tunnel vision," Cathy commented.

"That's right, and the news, especially the TV news, only

reports on war, famine or political uprisings. I can't remember seeing anything good on TV lately that would indicate that any place other than North America has something positive happening," Ruth said.

"Now you understand why I enjoyed travelling so much to other countries. I receive a first-hand view of what is happening, and I only go once or twice a year. The professional money manager is constantly in touch with and kept up-to-date on the countries where they have invested. Because Canada plays such a small part in the world economy, they must keep up to date on world events and how they effect us."

"What other types of mutual funds are there, Liz?" Ruth asked.

"You can buy a preferred stock fund, which is also considered an equity fund. This kind of fund generally pays a monthly dividend and still participates, to some extent, in the growth of the company. Preferred stock funds are a favourite of retired people who are looking for less risk and a steady stream of income. Another choice of the older person looking for income is the mortgage fund, which is not unlike a bond fund. This fund invests in a pool of mortgages and generates a monthly income as well. Because the manager generally invests in first mortgages or insured mortgages, this fund is viewed as a very conservative investment."

"What do you mean by insured mortgages?" Ruth asked.

"The National Housing Act states that certain mortgages must be insured in order to protect the lender in event of default by the borrower. The lender, in this case the mutual fund, would be reimbursed if the borrower failed to honour his mortgage commitment. So the mutual fund is protected from losses," Judy answered.

"Gee, that seems like a safe investment," Ruth said.

"Well, it is," Liz responded. "The only negative thing about a mortgage fund is that not unlike bonds and preferred shares, the price of a mortgage fund can fall when interest rates rise. Buying a fund like this when interest rates are high and holding it until interest rates decline is the best way to protect your capital. It is an excellent product for someone with a long time horizon who is looking for a better than average interest rate.

"Of course, we all know how bonds work, and you can buy a bond mutual fund. A bond fund is a good concept, because you are able to participate with other investors in what ultimately becomes a blended rate. The managers, with so much money to invest, stagger the maturities of the bonds. Some will be three-year, or five-year and so on, and depending on where we are in an interest rate cycle, they may buy a 30-year bond. Therefore, you the investor receive a blended rate of return from all of the investments. If interest rates are poised to rise, the manager may keep the maturities very short so the unit value doesn't drop as drastically as it would if they were invested in long-term bonds. That is the expertise that you are paying for."

"Can you invest in a bond issued by a foreign country or company?" Ruth asked.

"Yes, you can. There are two ways they do this. A Canadian bond issuer, like the government or a corporation, may issue the Canadian bond in a foreign currency, or you can purchase a foreign bond."

"Why would a Canadian company offer a bond in a different currency?" Cathy asked.

"Good question, Cathy. The company may be planning a major project in a foreign country or interest rates may be lower in a foreign country.

"The second way to invest is to buy bonds issued by a foreign country or corporation. A fund that invests in foreign bonds can be a very good investment, especially if interest rates in that country are high and due to come down," Liz said.

"But remember the currency risk!" Ruth reminded us.

"Yes, you should ask whether or not the fund manager hedges the currency in the fund. This strategy could cost the fund money, but it should protect the fund's currency exposure," Liz explained.

"What do you mean, cost the fund money?" Judy asked.

"They purchase a futures contract or possibly an option to lock in the value of the currency today. The option costs money in the form of a premium. The fund's capital, your money, is used to buy this contract, which is a direct cost to the fund and may reduce the return to the investors," she explained.

"So, what you are saying is that you give up a little in the overall return, but your risk of currency fluctuation is minimized," Ruth said, trying to get it clear in her head.

"Yes, this strategy is called hedging. The manager will buy a currency into the future to protect the fund in the event of a rising or falling dollar. Not unlike if you and I were going on vacation to England next year. If the British pound was low, you would buy it today, and hold it in case it goes up next year. Same principal," Liz explained.

"What about a gold fund, Liz," Annie inquired.

"A gold fund is a speciality fund, an industry distinction meaning it specializes in a particular segment of the market," Liz said.

"Doesn't that mean that a bond fund would be a speciality fund?" Cathy asked.

"A bond fund is a fundamental investment and not considered a speciality. It is more a basic core product. A gold fund would invest in gold stocks or bullion, which can be in the form of gold bars or certificates. Another speciality fund - a resource fund- would be invested in the oil and gas industry, and I would classify a real estate fund as a speciality fund. There aren't too many open-ended real estate funds left. The last recession really took its toll on this segment of the market. As most of these funds actually hold buildings in their portfolios, they can be very illiquid. If more shareholders want to redeem than the fund has cash to pay, the manager can't chip a piece off a building and raise cash. And if the building won't sell, he's got a problem. Remember I said in the beginning the fund guarantees to buy back your shares, but if it doesn't have any cash, it can't. Most of these open-ended funds became closed-end mutual funds during 1993, which is what they should have been in the first place. The real estate funds that invested in traded shares of companies that own real estate fared much better, and because they can sell the underlying security in the stock market, they still operate as open-ended funds. This situation has happened before and will probably happen again in the future."

"Liz, I saw an ad for a 'green fund.' Is that an environmental fund?" Cathy asked.

"In the past few years new funds have appeared that put very restrictive rules in place as to what type of company they'll invest in," Liz explained. "And yes, they are referred to as 'green funds,' or 'environmental funds.' Some may also be referred to as 'ethical funds'. Their managers will only invest in companies that are socially responsible."

"I think that is a great concept, Liz, especially for the adults of the future, as the schools are becoming so environmentally aware today," Cathy mentioned.

"Yes, it is an interesting concept. The fund may choose not to invest in a country where racial discrimination is prevalent or in a company that is not environmentally focused. This type of fund may not invest in a company that derives a major part of its income from tobacco products or is involved with nuclear energy. They have successfully attracted many investors in their niche market because all of us have become so environmentally aware over the past 10 years or so. The government can impose heavy fines on companies that do not bring their operations up to the current standards, so the bottom line of some companies can be affected by broken or ignored environmental rules. By investing in environmentally responsible corporations, this out-side factor should be eliminated."

"What if you aren't comfortable investing in the stock market, Liz? Is there a fund available for someone like that?" Cathy asked.

"Yes. It is called a money market fund. It is the alternative to a savings account. The manager selects a variety of short-term investments, generally coming due within 180 days. A money market fund provides a blended rate of return, which generates income to the investor generally on a monthly basis, although there are a few money market funds that distribute their income weekly. The portfolio will consist of short-term debt, known as Treasury Bills or T-Bills, issued by the Government of Canada, or notes issued by a province. It may also include corporate paper issued by large corporations."

"I assume by corporate paper your not referring to toilet paper printed with the company's logo," Annie said.

"Sorry," Liz said laughing. "You guys have become so knowledgeable that I forgot for a moment that I wasn't dealing with experts. Forgive me, corporate paper or commercial paper are notes issued by corporations or finance companies and they are not unlike a T-Bill. They are sold at a discount to the face value and mature within a year. Because they are issued by companies rather than by governments they generally offer a better return."

"Thank you, for clarifying that," Annie said.

"Now getting back to money market funds," Liz said still laughing. "Some invest strictly in T-Bills, but a better rate of return is earned if the manager is allowed to buy other vehicles, like commercial paper. Each fund outlines their investment policy in the prospectus, and almost every management company offering a family of funds will offer a money market product. There are over 100 money market funds in Canada and once you have a small reserve in a savings account, the next portion of your savings should be in a money-market fund."

"Do they pay more than a savings account and are they insured?"

"No insurance, Cathy, but they are safe. They are backed, as I explained earlier, by the issuer of the investments the fund holds. Most money market funds invest in T-Bills which are issued by the government. Money market funds certainly pay more than savings accounts and generally more than short-term GICs, and some of the money market funds offer chequing privileges."

"You mean that I would receive a cheque book and be able to simply write a cheque, and draw on my money market fund?" Cathy tried to clarify.

"That's right. There is a fee charged for this service, and it is usually more expensive than writing a cheque on your bank account, but it is a very convenient way to keep your money working continuously, while still allowing you quick access," Liz replied.

"Can a business use a money market fund?" Annie asked.

"Yes, and should, if they have excess cash say for 30 days or more. Why do you ask Annie?"

"Well I know that on occasion Mark's business has a fair amount of excess cash and he just leaves it sitting in the current account earning nothing," she responded.

"If that's the case, he should investigate a money market fund and look for one with chequeing privileges. That way, if his company needs the cash quickly, they just write a cheque," Liz said.

"That's a great concept. My savings account is hardly paying anything. I'm going to look into that right away," I said.

"There are U.S. dollar money market funds as well, which pay a better return than the banks, generally. Snowbirds heading to the U.S. in the winter use them rather than converting their cash back and forth each spring and fall."

"Liz, what if you are unable to make a decision on which fund to buy or if you are just not confident in making the right decision. What then?" Ruth asked.

"Good question, Ruth. There are two types of strategy funds available: the balanced fund and the asset allocation fund.

"Asset allocation funds and balanced funds eliminate the decision-making process that an investor must go through when deciding which type of fund to buy. Even with all of the knowledge we've gained, for some, this may still be a problem. These funds also eliminate decisions about when to buy. It can be as important to be in the right investment at the right time as it is to pick the right investment.

"With both types of fund, portfolio managers will strategically move from one area of the market to another. Depending on where we are in a business cycle, they may invest mostly in stocks, or if interest rates are high and stock market sluggish, they have the ability to move the money into bonds, enabling the fund to take advantage of a possible downward trend in interest rates. There may be times when the only place to be is in cash.

"There is, however, a major difference between the balanced fund and the asset allocation fund. It is unlikely that a balanced fund would ever be invested 100 percent in any one area, that is, 100 percent money market or 100 percent bonds or equities. As the name suggests, it takes a more balanced approach, with a portion invested in each area all the time.

"On the other hand, an asset allocation fund may be 100 percent in the money market or in equities or bonds, wherever the manager feels is the right place to be at a particular time. This fund is an excellent choice for the first-time investor, as it eliminates the fear of making the wrong choice. I like this concept, because unlike most equity or bond funds which concentrate in one area and are generally at least 80 percent invested all the time, managers of an asset allocation fund, if they are correct when making decisions, can protect your assets in a declining market."

"Yes, that makes sense to me," Cathy said.

"Liz, what are segregated funds?" Ruth asked. "There is a whole section of them in the paper."

"A segregated fund is offered only through the insurance industry and is basically the same as any other open-ended mutual fund, with a few exceptions. The insurance industry is governed under a different Act, and it requires that the investor be guaranteed a percentage of their investment regardless of what it is worth. The guarantee states that if the investment is held for a specific length of time, the insurance company will guarantee the return from of 75 to 100 percent of the initial investment upon redemption. This approach tends to make the investment very conservative as the manager has a liability to the shareholders if the fund falls drastically."

"You mean that if my segregated mutual fund was down 60 percent I would receive 75 percent of my initial investment back?" Ruth questioned.

"Yes, provided that you had had that particular investment for, say, 10-years," Liz responded.

"That seems like a good deal."

"Yes, but you shouldn't choose an investment just because of a guarantee. Somewhere along the line you are paying for that guarantee, whether it is in higher fees or in performance. I have never heard anyone brag that they received 75 percent of their investment back after 10 years."

"Maybe they did during the stock market crash in '29," Ruth said.

"These types of investments weren't available then."

"Well, Liz, you've certainly laid out our choices for us," Judy said. "How do we select the right manager?"

"I think you have to trust your investment advisor," Liz said.

"But what if you wanted to buy from a bank or trust company?" Annie asked. "How would you know which managers are the best?"

"You'd have to do your homework. First of all, you must check the past five and 10-year performance figures, but ensure that the person in charge of the fund today is the same one who was responsible for the historical performance. Make sure you read and understand the prospectus. Understand exactly what the manager is investing in and what restrictions, if any, are imposed on the fund. The problem as I see it, is continuing to monitor when the company makes any changes to the management of the fund."

"Would my branch know that?" Ruth asked.

"Yes, I suspect they would, and in addition, the bank's mutual fund departments all have toll free numbers, so you can call to get the information."

"Liz, if we invest through a financial advisor, a specialist, would they call us if something major changed at the fund?" Cathy inquired.

"Yes, that is what you are paying them to do. They should be monitoring your investments all along."

"Well, I'm not capable of researching all of these companies. I'm going to get a financial advisor," Annie said.

"I think you are wise. There are over 1,000 investment funds in Canada and it requires constant monitoring of the industry and market conditions to maintain an investment portfolio. It can be a full-time job, and unless you are very sophisticated, selecting an investment on your own can be dangerous."

"How do I find a good financial advisor?"

"I have been thinking about that, Annie, and there are many ways to go about it. Maybe you have a friend or a relative who could recommend one, or you could look in the yellow pages under Investment Advisors or Dealers. If you called one of these firms, they would give you a name and set up an appointment. You would then interview the person and if you are comfortable, you are on your way. But I think one of the best ways to select a financial advisor is to attend one of the many financial seminars that are advertised in the newspaper," Liz offered.

"Actually, I just received a flyer in the mail yesterday. It is an invitation to a seminar on Tuesday night, being held at that new hotel at the corner. If you want, I'll call and reserve some seats," Judy offered.

"I think that's a great idea. This way you'll be able to meet the representatives, in addition to hearing what they have to say," Liz suggested.

"As I recall, this particular seminar is focusing on international investing," Judy explained.

"I think you'll all enjoy it. It'll expose you to the company and the financial advisor without having to make a commitment, and you'll pick up great information. I believe at this stage that you all are knowledgeable enough to really benefit from this kind of seminar and maybe you'll feel comfortable enough to do business with the sponsors of the meeting."

"Ok, I'm free Tuesday night, so I'll go," Annie said.

"Yes. Everybody is nodding, so I'll make the arrangements," Judy agreed. "What about you, Liz?"

"Thank you very much, but you are on you're own. I think it'll be better if I don't go."

"Well, I guess it's time to call it a day," I said.

"We are certainly making good progress," Liz said confidently. "Next month, we'll be focusing on RRSPs, and once we understand those you should be ready to make your investment choices."

"Who received the RRSP book for Christmas?" Annie asked.

"I did," Cathy replied.

"Can I borrow it for a few days, please?" Annie asked.

"I'll bring it over tomorrow, Annie."

"Great, I'm on my way. See you all Tuesday night. Bye Liz."

Chapter Six
February

It was an unusually sunny day for February. There was no wind and the night's snowfall had a cleansing effect on the neighbourhood. It was one of those days when we're fooled into thinking that winter really is the best season of the year.

"Tell me about the seminar," Liz inquired, as she scooped some delicious shrimp spread onto a cracker. We enjoy meeting at Ruth's because she lovingly prepares many of the canapes she has been serving her guests over the years.

"It was an excellent presentation. The evening was sponsored by a large mutual fund company and one of the portfolio managers explained the reasons we should be investing in emerging markets. He talked about developments in South America, what is happening in the Middle East and explained the political problems of China. I learned so much in just two hours, it was great!" Ruth exclaimed.

"I learned a lot as well. But you know, Liz, I would have been totally lost and probably bored had you not been preparing us," Annie said.

"I'm pleased that you found the evening valuable. Did you meet a representative who you feel you might be able to work with?"

"I think I did," Annie said. "We lingered after the presentation was over, talking and having a coffee, and one of the financial advisors came over, asked if we had any questions and if we had enjoyed the presentation. He appeared very knowledgeable and we told him how impressed we were with the portfolio manager. He said that this particular manager had been with the company for 15 years and , Doug, that's his name, said he had been placing his clients with this portfolio manager for years, in another fund that he also managed. Just as you said, Liz, this portfolio manager is originally from Brazil, which is why he was chosen to manage this new fund which concentrates on South America. Anyway, Doug says he is one of the top money managers around and that he should do extremely well for the investors."

"Yes, I was impressed by Doug as well," Judy said. "We told him what we are doing and that we wouldn't be ready to make a decision until later this month. He gave us his telephone number and told us to call him when we are ready."

"That's great. But you know, there are many seminars at this time of year and I think that you should go to another."

"I agree," Cathy said. "I think I'll continue looking. In fact, there is an RRSP seminar next Thursday that I think I'll attend."

"We'll go with you, right?" said Ruth turning to the rest of us.

"Yes, we'll go, it won't hurt to shop around," Judy said.

"I'm feeling so smug about what we've learned over the past

few months," Ruth stated. "I have such a feeling of comfort knowing that I have a power of attorney in place and my stock is doing so well. I feel great!"

"What stock?" Annie asked.

"Well, you remember the $5,000 Bob gave me to invest? I called his broker, Bud. He's been advising Bob for years. I invested in a computer company and in less than a month it is up $1.50."

"I don't believe this, we have a female Donald Trump in our midst," Annie quipped. "I thought the closer you were to retirement, the safer your investments should be. Should you really be playing the stock market, Ruth?"

"You are making a couple of assumptions here, Annie," Liz said. "First, Ruth and I talked about the investment before she made her choice and the $5,000 does not represent all of Ruth's assets. Also, it makes proper investing sense to have some of your money invested in the stock market. The allocated percentage is the important factor to determine as you come closer to retirement. By not investing in the equity market you take the chance that inflation will outpace your capital. Certainly someone of Ruth's age should not have all of their money directly in the stock market, but there is nothing wrong with having a small percentage. Ruth understands the risk and we'll keep our eyes on the progress of the company. And secondly, when you research a company as thoroughly as Ruth did, you can hardly refer to her investment as 'playing.'"

"That's right. When I first talked to Bud, I learned that his firm had already written a report on the computer company that I was interested in."

"You mean, you called him and you told him what stock you wanted to buy?" Annie asked, surprised.

"Yes, we held a dinner party last month and one of Bob's clients was talking about this company," Ruth explained. "You know, for years I disliked our dinner parties. I always felt that once I had the meal on the table, my job was done. I had never been comfortable participating in the conversations. But with my new-found knowledge, I quite enjoyed the whole evening and you should have seen Bob when I started to question his client about this company. I sensed that he was uncomfortable at first - after all this was the first time that I had participated in the business conversation. Our dinner guest was most willing to share everything he knew about this company. Bob said later that he was surprised at my interest and even more amazed at my understanding of the market. I was really excited about the information, and on Monday morning I called Bud. I asked him, just as Liz had taught us, what the price to earnings ratio was, and what the high and low price of the stock had been during the past 12 months. Both the ratio and price were low. That, coupled with the news that the company has developed a new software package which has been well received by the business community, enabled me to make my decision. The company has been in business for 16 years and this is the third successful product that they have developed. I'm very optimistic that they are going to do very well in the future."

"I'm surprised at you, Ruth, and also a little envious," Annie stated. "But I would be terrified that the stock would go down and I would lose all my money."

"I think that would be a valid concern, Annie. If it were all your money, you should be terrified. But a large, properly structured portfolio of investments should contain some stock."

"What if the market crashes like it did in 1987?" Annie continued.

"It'll come back," Liz replied. "Even if the market does decline, it doesn't mean that the company will go out of business, and if Ruth doesn't sell the stock if it drops in price, she only has a paper loss, which will change daily. If the fundamentals of the company are good, she'll be fine. The mistake that investors make is becoming panicky and selling their stock when the price is down. It is these same investors who'll buy when the price is too high. This is a good investment and I think Ruth will double her money over the next few years."

"We are going to be watching your stock, Ruth," Annie warned.

"I'm not the only one who bought this stock. Liz did as well," Ruth said defensively.

"Yes, I did. I think that it is a good investment, but I bought it in my RRSP," Liz explained, reaching for more canapes.

"Speaking about RRSPs Liz, there is so much advertising on TV and through the mail about RRSPs now. I've never bought one because of my teacher's pension plan. Do you think that I should?" Cathy asked.

"Definitely, Cathy. You should take advantage of the tax deduction. This is the RRSP season. The deadline being 60 days after the year end makes February RRSP month. The office is so busy this time of year that I can't convince any of my old friends who still work at the company to take an hour to join me for lunch. Clients traditionally wait until the last month and in some cases, the last minute to make their contribution. It is a crazy time of year for anyone involved in RRSPs."

"We're not as busy this year," Judy said. "Interest rates are so low that people are not locking their money in GICs as they have in the past."

"That's right, everybody is investing their RRSPs in the equity market, so the pressure is on the financial advisors."

"Explain to me, please, why I should have one, Liz. I am so young and I can't even think about retiring at this stage of my life. I can't believe that I need one," Annie said.

"If you don't start now, Annie, you'll be missing out on the best deal in Canada. No other country in the world is as liberal with their retirement option as Canada is. You should have opened one the first year you started earning money. Retirement sneaks up on you and you can't imagine the peace of mind you'll have, knowing that you are taking care of your future."

"You are so right, Liz," Ruth stated. "I can't imagine that Bob and I are going to retire in two years. It seems like only last year that the boys were still home. It is like an unseen force pushing me rapidly into old age and I don't want to go. Actually, I didn't want to go from the age of 40."

"What do you mean the best deal in Canada?" Annie asked.

"Annie, if I said to you I'll give you $40 for each $100 you save, would you do it?"

"Of course!" she exclaimed.

"Well, that's exactly what the government is saying to you when you deposit into your RRSP. You'll receive a tax refund based on whatever tax bracket you are in. If you are in a 30 percent tax bracket for each $100 you put in your RRSP you would receive $30, $40 if you are in the 40 percent bracket, and $50 if you are in the 50 percent bracket. Smart people contribute their maximum amount and never touch it until they retire."

"But there are so many other considerations for someone my age, such as Brett's education or an emergency. We may want to have another baby and hopefully, Mark's business will be profitable soon and I'll be able to stop working until the kids are in school. I can't look to retirement when there is so much else going on," Annie replied.

"I disagree," Liz said. "If you have a savings program today, after you have enough money set aside for an emergency, you should put the rest into a RRSP. Annie, what is the worst financial circumstance that could happen to you?"

She thought for a moment and said, "I guess if I lost my job."

"Okay, let's say that for the past five years you had been putting $3,000 each year into your RRSP and you lost your job. You would have received at least a $1,200 tax refund for each year that you contributed, that's $1,200 times five which equals $6,000 you have also set aside. You can dip into the $6,000 first, and if you are still unemployed and require additional funds, you can then withdraw some or all of the money in your RRSP, which at this point in time should be worth say $20,000. You must pay tax when you withdraw any of the RRSP funds, but if you do it smartly, you can minimize the tax."

"I didn't realize that you could withdraw. I thought it was

locked in until you were 65 years old," Annie said.

"A number of people are under this assumption, and it is incorrect. The only time RRSP money is locked-in is when company pension money has been transferred to it. During the last recession, some people, in order to survive financially, had to dip into their retirement plan.

"An RRSP is such a critical part of savings, it amazes me that after all these years, so many people still aren't taking advantage of this vehicle. It is by far the best method of saving for your future years. All of the income earned in the plan is tax sheltered until you withdraw it, at which time it becomes taxable, earned income, just like you were still working, but of course, you should then be in a lower income bracket. In addition to that, and one of the best features, you are using money which ordinarily would be paid to the government to increase your retirement plan. Because untaxed compounding is such an important feature of long-term savings, you are using the government's money to enhance your RRSP."

"So where do we buy an RRSP?" Cathy asked.

"First, you don't buy an RRSP. You open a plan, into which you deposit your contribution and then invest the money. You can open one at almost any financial institution: a bank, trust company, insurance company, credit union, brokerage firm or directly with a mutual fund company. All of them offer RRSPs," Liz responded.

"Who determines what investments can be put into an RRSP, Liz?" Cathy asked.

"Revenue Canada sets the rules and outlines what is and is not eligible for an RRSP," Liz replied.

"And what is the best investment to buy in your RRSP?" Cathy continued with her questioning.

"The list of investments is quite extensive and you might want to invest differently each year, depending on the market conditions. Because your RRSP is a long-term investment plan, age plays a critical role when making your choice. Also, looking at the business cycle to see at what stage it is at is important. If interest rates are high, you might want to put some money into a term deposit or a bond or bond mutual fund. All of the investments that we have discussed up to this point can be purchased in an RRSP. However, some may have restrictions as to the maximum percentage allowed," Liz stated.

"Liz, I mentioned to you earlier that I have Canada Savings Bonds. Can I put some of them into an RRSP?" I asked.

"Yes, Barb, and you should, because at present every dollar of interest that you earn on your bond is fully taxed. You should contribute them to an RRSP. I assume that you are in a high tax bracket, Barb, and you should put your maximum amount in immediately."

"When I receive my final income tax assessment from Revenue Canada, there is a dollar amount in the RRSP line. Is that how much I may put in?" I asked.

"Yes, if you have not contributed to an RRSP. The government keeps track of how much you are allowed to contribute and you can deposit it in all at once, reducing your taxable income substantially. You are able to carry forward unused contribution amounts for seven years. I'll give you an example.

"If someone earned enough for five years to put in $10,000 each year and hadn't, in the sixth year they would be able to contribute $50,000. If our hypothetical person earned $75,000 in year six, a contribution of $50,000 could be made. This would effectively reduce their earned income from $75,000 to $25,000. This person should receive a very large refund although they might be subject to the Alternative Minimum Tax, which prevents high income earners from reducing their income tax below a specified amount."

"Boy, wouldn't a big refund be nice!" Annie said.

"Yes, but the problem is that they have lost all the years of compounding and the sheltering of income, and it is smarter to reduce your income each year rather than all at once. It is not the best strategy, but at least today you don't lose the right to make up those lost years, as we did a few years ago," Liz stated.

"I would also think, Liz, that they would risk the government changing the rules," Judy cautioned.

"That's right, Judy. Any of these rules can be changed at any time. You know it is the old story that a bird in the hand is worth two in the bush."

"How do I contribute Canada Savings Bonds? Do I have to cash them in?" I asked.

"No, you must open a self-directed RRSP and the trustee will deposit the bonds to your plan. If you bought your bonds, for example, two years ago, you'll be required to include the income earned to date on your tax return. You must pay tax on that portion. The financial institution will issue a tax reporting form which will show the interest amount to be included on your income tax return. If the face value of the bonds was $10,000 and the interest accumulated from the date you bought them until the day you contribute them to your RRSP was $2,500, you would be required to pay tax on the $2,500 but would receive an RRSP contribution receipt for $12,500. Any interest earned from the date that you deposited them to your RRSP would be income earned in the plan and would be sheltered. The same thing applies to all investments. Any investment made to the plan, in kind, which is what this transaction is referred to, must be made at the market or current value on the day of contribution."

"Liz, you mean that if I wanted to contribute my stock which is now worth $6,500, I would have to pay tax on the $1,500 that it has increased in value so far?" Ruth asked.

"Yes, Ruth. You paid $5,000 for it, and if you wanted to deposit it to your RRSP, you would receive a contribution receipt for $6,500 and would be required to pay capital gains tax on the $1,500," Liz said.

"Even though I haven't sold it? What if the stock was worth less than what I paid for it when I decided to contribute it?"

"When you transfer investments to an RRSP for tax purposes it is considered a sale even though you technically still own it, and you must pay tax on a capital gain. However, if when you contributed your stock it was only worth $4,000, you would not be able to take a loss on the $1,000."

"Why?" asked Annie.

"It is just one of those tax rules that all Canadians must abide by," Liz responded.

"Bob has so many different RRSPs because he has been contributing for years, and they are all over the place, at different institutions. It takes days to figure out what he has and where it is and as soon as he seems to have it all together, another statement comes in and throws him for a loop. How can we simplify this process, Liz?" Ruth asked.

"This is a common problem for someone who has been contributing for a long time, Ruth. He is not alone. Every year most people run at the last minute to the bank or trust company offering the highest interest rate, make their contribution and forget about it until it comes due a few years later, generally five years. Bob should consolidate all of his plans under one roof in a self-directed RRSP, but let's start at the beginning.

"The thinking for years has been that an RRSP is sacred and should never be exposed to risk, that the only investment in an RRSP should be safe, interest-bearing vehicles because the income is sheltered from tax. This approach is wrong - it really is a myth. Think of all of your assets as your complete portfolio. In fact the goal should be to properly diversify your holdings, take advantage of a balanced portfolio and again, depending on your age, ensure that the investments are such that they have the opportunity to grow. For example, you Annie, being so young, should be investing in an aggressive equity mutual fund, because you have a long time horizon before you need it. For the next three years you should contribute to one or two different funds. Each mutual fund company offers their own RRSP, but are restricted to their investments only. After three or four years and when you have accumulated at least $10,000, you should then transfer to a self-directed plan, which will allow you to move within the plan to take advantage of changing times as quickly and easily as possible. You see, if you want to buy a different investment at a different institution and your plans are spread all over the place, like Bob's, it can be quite a time-consuming effort to transfer the money, not to mention that he is probably paying each institution a fee. You'll have to go to a new institution and open a new plan, complete a transfer form, ensure that it is sent to the old trustees and wait until the transfers are completed before you can make the new investment. Depending on the time of year and how busy these institutions are, you could be facing weeks of delays. When you have a self-directed plan, you instruct your institution or financial advisor to sell one investment and buy another, and you pay only one trustee fee. It is just that easy." Liz explained.

"So a self-directed plan eliminates all that running around. And when you transfer from one institution to another I'll bet you can't buy the new investment until the money arrives and probably by then the price or rate could have changed, right, Liz?" Ruth asked.

"Exactly. In addition, you are earning nothing on the money while it is in transit, and on large amounts this can add up. Barb, if you intended to make up your carry-forward this year, I would suggest that you open a self-directed plan right away."

"What is the fee for an RRSP, Liz," I asked.

"A self-directed plan will generally cost $100 to $125 each year, which is tax deductible if, when you open your plan, you tell the trustee that you want to pay your fee outside of your plan. You'll then be billed. Some trustees will take it out of your bank account directly and you'll receive a tax receipt which will allow you to deduct the cost from your income tax. If the fee is paid from money inside the RRSP, you can't deduct it.

"Ensure also that you designate a beneficiary on your plan when you open it. Ruth, you should check to see that Bob has named you the beneficiary on all of his plans. A spouse or a dependent, disabled child or grandchild are the only people to whom a plan can be transferred upon death without being taxed."

"A common law spouse now has the same rights as a legal wife for tax purposes," Judy stated.

"Oh, that's good for you, Judy," Cathy said. "That at least will help protect you with Paul."

"You are right, Cathy, but I don't think that'll be a concern for me in the future. Paul's ex-wife is terminally ill and has been hospitalized. They have three teenagers still at home and Paul is going back to take care of the kids, so I'll be alone again."

"I'm so sorry, Judy," said Ruth. "What an unusual situation."

"Yes, it is. We found out last week. She was taken ill suddenly and is deteriorating very fast. Actually, I admire his commitment to the children."

"Why don't they all move in with you, or you with them?" Ruth asked.

"Quite frankly, Ruth, I've raised my children. I don't think that I have the energy or desire to take on the responsibility of three teenagers. The only other alternative was to uproot the children in the middle of the school year and move them to their grandmother's. What Paul is doing is a much more sensible approach and I am proud that he has stepped up to the plate and is taking on the responsibility, but it still hurts."

"I'll bet it does," Cathy stated. "As I remember, you rent your house, don't you? Are you going to be able to manage?"

"I think so, but it's too early to tell. This is why I didn't say anything. I didn't want to break our focus in these sessions, so maybe we should just get back to the RRSP."

"Okay, but if there is anything any of us can do, just let us know," Liz offered.

"Thank you," Judy said.

"What types of investments would you recommend for my RRSP, Liz? Remember that I have a good teacher's pension," Cathy inquired.

"Well, I assume you are in your mid-40s, Cathy, so you have 20 or so years to continue working. That and the fact that you have such a good pension should allow you to be fairly aggressive. My advice to you would be the same as to Annie. The closer you get to retirement, the more conservative your investments, but you have a long time to go before retirement. You have at least four or five business cycles to take advantage of, so don't be afraid to be aggressive. Ruth is the one who should be fairly conservative.

"Ruth, if Bob has been contributing to his RRSPs in his name all of these years, it is imperative that he begin making spousal contributions to your plan this year and each year until he retires. This will provide you with a little pension of your own and it allows income splitting."

"What do you mean by income splitting?" Ruth asked.

"The aim of income splitting is to create two incomes and if you are in different tax brackets, it'll result in a tax saving."

"That's a great idea," Ruth responded.

"A spousal plan should have been established for you years ago, Ruth. Couples should make sure that RRSP contributions are divided equally between their two plans."

"Is this a common practice, Liz?" Cathy asked.

"Yes it is. Some people are concerned about the assets in an RRSP due to the possibility of a marital breakdown. But in the event of a divorce, most provinces now provide for all marital assets to be split evenly including the RRSP and pensions. Also, you must be careful, because any contribution made to a spouse's RRSP is taxed back to the contributor if withdrawn within a three-year period of the last contribution."

"What if you don't have the money to put into an RRSP, Liz?" Annie asked.

"Annie, an RRSP is so important that if I didn't have the money, I would borrow it. A loan for an RRSP contribution should be paid back within a year. Let's say interest rates are 10 percent and you borrow $5,000. The cost of that loan would only be approximately $275 over the year. If you are in a 40 percent bracket your refund alone would be $2,000. You should look upon it as a forced savings, plus the benefit of sheltering all the income. And with the compounding effect, you are way ahead of the game," Liz explained.

"Yes, that makes sense to me. But if the interest on a loan is 10 percent, how can the cost of the loan only be $275? It should be $500 on a $5,000 loan," Annie questioned.

"The interest is charged on a declining balance because every monthly payment that you make reduces the outstanding balance and the interest is charged on the reduced amount," Judy said.

"That's right. The other way to ensure that your RRSP commitment is met is through monthly contributions," Liz suggested. "Most issuers of RRSPs will set up a PAC, which is a pre-authorized cheque, which allows the institution to automatically deduct a specified amount from your bank account every month and deposit it to your RRSP. This way you are not scrambling at the last minute to come up with the money. A similar arrangement can be set up through a group RRSP with your employer. Every pay period your employer deducts the amount from the your pay cheque and remits it to the trustee for credit to your plan."

"Yes, this arrangement has an additional feature, in that the income tax deduction is less, so in essence you receive your refund immediately," Judy added.

"Yes, that's right," Liz confirmed.

"You lost me," Annie said puzzled.

"If you are in a 40 percent tax bracket and you want to have $500 a month deducted from your salary as an RRSP contribution, the tax, $200, which would ordinarily be remitted on that $500, is not withheld. The employer deducts the $500 for your RRSP and remits $200 less to the government which decreases your net pay only $300 instead of the $500," Liz explained.

"That's a great concept. Why doesn't every employer do this?" Annie exclaimed.

"I think I'll propose this concept to my staff. Is it a lot of work for the employer?" I asked. "I don't want to create an administrative nightmare."

"No. Once it is in place it is very simple to administer, much easier than a pension plan, and some employers use it as a bonus plan as well, by also contributing and matching the employee's amount," Liz said.

"Liz, based on what you have said today, I gather that you recommend mutual funds for RRSPs," Ruth commented.

"Yes, I do. They both represent, in most cases, a long time frame and because of this, they go together like bread and butter, salt and pepper, ice cream and chocolate sauce."

"That did it," Ruth exclaimed, as she reached for the canapes.

"The other advantage of a mutual fund investment is the ease with which you can invest outside of Canada. Remember we talked about the advantages and disadvantages of the foreign markets, the disadvantages being the volatility and the difficult buying directly in a foreign country? With mutual funds offering so many different investments outside of Canada, they are a good place to take advantage of the opportunity to expose your RRSP to the foreign markets. Because RRSPs are a long-term concept, it removes the pressure of the volatile conditions."

"Can you invest in U.S. dollars in an RRSP? It seems to me that because so many people travel to the warm part of the states when they retire, this would be a good idea for some of their retirement funds," Ruth stated.

"Yes, actually you can. The RRSP investment rules are simple.

First ask, is the investment eligible and then ask, is it considered a foreign investment. Some mutual fund companies offer RRSP money market funds in U.S. dollars and some trust companies offer U.S. term deposits from one to five years. If you look in the paper there should be a symbol that tells you when a fund is offered in U.S. dollars and another that indicates whether it is 100 percent eligible. Most of the available investments are money market funds, but U.S. bond funds are available as well."

"Wouldn't they fall under the 20 percent rule for foreign investments?" Ruth asked.

"No, the act says that the investment must be through a Canadian issuer such as a Canadian mutual fund, a trust company, or bank. So as long as the issuer is Canadian, this type of investment should be eligible. If you purchased a U.S. investment from a U.S. issuer, in the form of a country fund or a U.S.-issued term deposit, it would fall under the 20 percent rule."

"I would think that if someone had been investing their RRSP years ago into U.S. dollars, they would have certainly done well, given the exchange rate today," Annie suggested.

"Not necessarily. The interest earned is generally lower than a Canadian dollar investment. The exchange rate would have made up the difference if you had purchased when the Canadian dollar was high. I believe the U.S. dollar investments are only used as a convenience," Liz said. "Again, that's part of the risk. I remember years ago when the Canadian dollar was worth more than the U.S.,"

"No! I can't imagine. You mean that when you went shopping our dollar bought even more and their prices were lower too? Wow, what a treat that would be," Annie said in surprise.

"Yes, times have certainly changed," Ruth said.

"Our prices were lower then as well, because so much of what we consume comes from the U.S. and when our dollar is lower, as it is now, anything that we import costs more."

"Liz, you and Judy have been referring to a 20 percent rule. Please explain that for me," Annie asked.

"When you buy a foreign investment in your RRSP, you must be careful not to exceed 20 percent of the cost of your plan. The government imposes a penalty of one percent per month on any amount over the 20 percent maximum rule," Liz stated.

"What do you mean by the cost?" Cathy asked. "The original deposit?"

"No, you must keep track of the original cost, the book value, of all of your investments in your RRSP, not the contribution amount, and 20 percent of that total amount per plan can be foreign. Cost is the actual dollar amount including commission paid. If you buy a stock, you add the commission to the price, and if it is a mutual fund with a front-end load, the cost is the total amount of your purchase, including commission."

"You mean, the computer stock that I bought cost me $5 per share and I bought 1,000 shares plus the $150 commission I paid, so my total cost is $5,150?" Ruth calculated.

"Yes, you've got it," Liz replied, "and when investing in a front-end load mutual fund, you use the gross amount. Even if you only ultimately invested $4,700 after the commission of $300, the cost would be $5,000," Liz stated.

"Hold it!" Annie challenged hoisting her arm in the air. "Why are you talking about commission on a mutual fund, and what is a front-end load, when I see no commission advertised in the paper?"

"There are a few ways that you can buy a mutual fund, Annie. The first way is directly from an investment manager who distributes directly to the public and doesn't charge commission. The banks and trust companies offer mutual funds with no commission.

"You can also invest with an independent fund manager through someone like Doug, a commissioned financial advisor who guides you with your selection and provides ongoing advice. There are many commission structures available. One is a front-end load where the commission is deducted up front and the balance is invested. You may also select what is referred to as deferred sales charge. A deferred sales charge allows the investor to purchase a fund, paying no commission up front, but if you decide to sell the investment prior to a specific period of time, a redemption fee is payable. When you purchase a deferred sales charge fund the financial advisor is paid by the manager. If you hold the investment until the expired time frame, you'll not pay any fees. You may also buy a fund offered by the independent managers called a no-load or low-load fund. With each one of these options the management fee charged is differently. It is important to take into account the annual management fee. If the fee has been increased by one-half or one percent on a no-load fund and you keep the investment for a long time, which you should do anyway, you may be better served by buying a deferred sales charge fund. You'll save money over the long term," Liz said. "Generally, the management fee through an independent manager is lowest on a front-end fund, and higher on a deferred load."

"Then why wouldn't I chose a front-end load to get the lower management fee?" Cathy asked.

"Because not all of your money is going to work for you immediately. Five or six percent will be deducted as commission."

"Why, if I can buy from a bank or a trust company and pay no commission, would I buy from someone like Doug?" Annie continued.

"I can answer that Annie," Judy said. "You have to ask yourself if a financial advisor adds value. If you are completely knowledgeable, you may not need someone like Doug. But because banks and trust companies don't yet provide a complete advisory service readily available to the investor, and with so many choices available, I really think that an investor, especially a new investor, needs guidance. Most people using a financial advisor don't have the time required to select and monitor their investments."

"That's right. Financial advisors like Doug are specialists in this area. It is not unlike going to a doctor. If you require a speciality service, you go to the specialist," Liz said.

"In addition, at a bank or trust company you are only able to purchase the investments that the bank or trust company manages," Judy added.

"You mean that if I go to my bank and want to buy a mutual fund offered by a manager not affiliated with the bank, I can't?" Cathy asked.

"That's right. The bank will refer you to their subsidiary

brokerage firm, if they have one. These firms have specialists who can offer you the same investments that Doug can. My former firm is now owned by a bank, and you would be directed to one of the brokers at the bank-owned firm," Liz explained.

"Are there other companies like bank and trust companies that only offer their products?" Annie asked.

"Yes. Insurance companies and some investment fund managers have their own sales force. This is referred to, in the industry, as a captive sales force."

"Is there anything wrong with buying from them?" she pushed.

"Absolutely not. They offer sound investment options, although they are restricted to their own products, not unlike the bank and trust company. I think one of the keys to investing is being comfortable with your advisor. If you have confidence in their ability to provide you with good sound advice, go ahead.

"If you select an investment manager who offers different types of investment options, like bond funds, mortgage funds, equity funds, international and domestic funds and money market funds, you can switch from one to another within the family and usually pay no commission. You really have the best of all worlds for your portfolio. And even if you do pay a commission, remember, few people have a problem adjusting to the fact that there is a commission on a stock purchase, which could cost more than buying a mutual fund."

"What do you mean?" Ruth asked. "And now you tell me!"

"Let's compare your stock investment to a front-end load

mutual fund. You stated that you paid $5,150 or $150 commission, that's a three percent commission, which is standard. Let's also assume that the value of your stock two years later is $10,000 and you want to sell. The selling commission would be three percent or $300, plus the $150 that you initially paid, which totals $450. If you purchased a front-end load mutual fund with the $5,000, the cost would probably be approximately five percent of the original price or $250 and you would not pay on the $10,000 value when you sell it. If you bought a fund with a deferred sales charge it is entirely possible that you would never pay a commission."

"I understand now. Thanks, Liz," Annie said.

"So it really costs more to buy a stock," Ruth stated.

"In most cases, yes. You can also buy and sell a stock and a mutual fund and pay less commission through a discount broker, who is basically an order taker and provides no advice whatsoever."

"I don't think that I am ready to invest without advice," Cathy stated. "I not only want advice, I want ongoing guidance."

"Cathy, because most mutual funds are sold to investors through a sales force, the fund manager pays a representative a trailer fee of generally one-quarter to one-half percent and sometimes higher, of his clients' assets. This trailer fee is paid to the selling firm to ensure that, while the client is still invested, the representative continues to service the client. This fee is charged and calculated in the manager's annual fee."

"This sounds like a good business to get into," Annie said. "Maybe I should be selling mutual funds, rather than working for my company."

"You can earn good money, and the industry certainly can use more women, but you have to be able to survive on commission, because there is no guaranteed salary."

"Good point. I must have the same or more money coming in every month as I do now or we don't make our mortgage payment," Annie replied.

"Actually, women make good investment counsellors and after you have developed your clientele, you can earn a good living, but it can take years to accomplish this."

"Women do make good advisors and teachers just look at ours, she's great!" Ruth declared.

"Thank you," Liz said, obviously embarrassed.

"Well, we're coming to the end of today's lesson, and I want to make sure that you understand everything so far, because I want each of you to open an RRSP before March 1, which is the deadline this year."

"I am going to have to borrow. How do I calculate how much I can put in?" Annie asked.

"Go back and find your income tax assessment notice from the government, it'll tell you. Subject to a maximum, the rule now is 18 percent of your previous year's earned income (earned income is different than investment income) less a pension adjustment if you belong to pension plan or a deferred-profit sharing plan. Cathy, you and Judy will be the only ones affected by this because you both have pension plans. If any of you have a carry-forward amount, I suggest that you take advantage of it and contribute the full amount. Annie, if you have to borrow, I would call Doug as soon as possible. He can arrange a loan for you. But don't leave it until the last minute. You should do it tomorrow. It is the middle of February already and it takes time to process a loan," Liz suggested. "Ruth, what are you going to do?"

"I'm going to make sure Bob's contribution is a spousal one this year," she responded.

"Good. Barb, what about you?"

"I'm going to find my assessment form and make up my carry-forward. I'll open a self-directed plan and deposit my Canada Savings Bonds. Once they are in place, I'll make my investment choice."

"What about you, Cathy." Liz inquired.

Cathy said, "I am going to open an RRSP. I'll have to look at my assessment as well to see how much I can contribute. I think I'll put my contribution into a money market fund for now."

"Good idea. You don't have to make an investment decision immediately, just make sure you deposit to an RRSP before the deadline.

"What about you, Judy? Your company offers RRSPs and you should be able to select one, no problem."

"Actually, Liz, I have been contributing a small amount every year for the past 10 years. It has added up, but I intend to put my maximum in this year and I would like to transfer it, from my company to an independent manager. I am considering this only because I don't think it is a good idea for my employer to know my financial business. Right now my whole RRSP is with my company."

"I think that is a wise decision, Judy."

As we began the process of piling on our winter gear, I heard Liz say to Judy, "If you need any help, Judy, give me a call, even if it is just to talk. I am sure this is going to be a lonely time. I'm really sorry that Paul is leaving."

"Thank you, I will," she replied sadly.

"Good-bye everyone, see you next month," Ruth said, as she closed the door.

It was only 4:30 in the afternoon but it was pitch dark.

Chapter Seven
March

It is hard to believe that spring officially begins in March. Whoever created the calendar didn't take Canada into consideration. The snowfalls appeared endless and our meeting had to be postponed twice. The first meeting caught two of us stranded away from home and the second cancellation was due to an ice storm that took the power out for hours. No wonder we are viewed as a hardy race of people. To survive Canadian winters requires diligence, dedication and, strong will.

It was the worst March I had ever experienced. The real estate market had all but ceased to exist. It was simply too cold to go out looking at houses. If the phone rang more than 10 times from 9 a.m. to 6 p.m. we considered it a busy day. I looked forward to our gathering just to be able to interact with people and since it was being held at my house, it meant that I didn't have to go out.

The others arrived one at a time over a period of 15 minutes or so and we settled down, snuggled as close to the fireplace as possible.

"I thought I would treat us today with hot chocolate with a very fattening cream topping sprinkled with cinnamon," I offered.

"And it is perfect, Barb," Anne said, licking the white cream moustache which had formed on her upper lip. "I have never been as cold as I have over the past few weeks. When will it stop? I can't take any more."

"Can we hold these meetings in Florida or a sunny island somewhere?" Ruth asked.

"Actually, I just saw an ad in the paper promoting a cruise where various seminars are held while you are at sea. You can attend all or some of them and learn about all kinds of things, including investments," Judy stated excitedly.

"Wouldn't it be marvellous to be sitting in the sun with a tall, cool drink and learning as we have been. Let's go!" Annie dreamed.

"Here's a thought. I just happen to have available to me, in a few weeks, a three-bedroom condominium in Palm Beach, Florida. You are all more than welcome to fly down next month and we can hold our session in the sun," I offered.

"What a great idea, do you think it is possible?" Judy asked.

"Bob would never let me go," Ruth declared.

"What do you mean, 'wouldn't let you go.' You never know until you ask," Annie said. "I am due for a week off and my mother is going to visit her sister. I think it would be a good opportunity for Mark to take care of Brett for a week. In fact, it would be a great experience," she laughed. "I'm going home and *tell* him that we are going."

"We could learn about the U.S investment world while we are

away," I said, trying to find an excuse for them.

"Maybe we could write the trip off on our income tax as an educational expense," Annie quipped.

"Somebody better check with an accountant on that one, but I'm game," Judy said. "I need a rest. Paul moved out two weeks ago and I think a vacation in Florida is just what I need to get things back in perspective."

"How are you making out, Judy?" Ruth asked. "It must be quite an adjustment living in that big house alone."

"I'm fine, actually, better than I thought I would be. My sons have been over for the first time in months and I have enjoyed the quiet time. I'm adjusting quite nicely, thank you, but I do have a question," she said.

"What is it?" Liz asked.

"I have some money from my late husband's estate and I find that I am going to have to draw on some of it in order to keep up with the monthly expenses. Paul and I split the rent and household expenses and with him gone, it is either move, which I don't want to do, or tap into my savings to stay in the house. My question, Liz, is, is there another way, rather than just drawing down my savings to supplement my income without going through all of my cash?"

"Have you thought about buying the house?" I asked.

"No, I haven't and I don't know whether or not it is for sale, but I think that I have enough money tucked away that I could manage most of it."

"The only problem I see with buying the house is the possible return of Paul," Liz said. "If, in the future, something happened again to the relationship, under certain circumstances, you could be at risk of losing half of your money. I would check with a lawyer before doing that."

"There is an investment plan, which is ideal for this situation, called a withdrawal plan. It is available with most mutual funds."

"What's that, Liz?" Annie asked.

"It's a great concept and I think it is one that you should look at, Judy."

"Okay, explain it please," Judy said.

"Let's say that we are talking about an investment of $200,000. You open a withdrawal plan account at one of the top money management firms and you then request that they send you a specific dollar amount every month until further notice. Let's say that you wanted to receive $2,000 a month. They would redeem the $2,000 from the fund and deposit it into your bank account. Now $2,000 a month for 12 months is $24,000, and that represents 12 percent of the initial investment. If the manager could produce an average return of slightly better than 12 percent on the investment, you would still have your capital in addition to supplementing your cash flow. If the manager produced a return much greater than 12 percent, your money would grow. And in the early years, the money you received would generally be considered a return of your own money rather than taxable income."

"That's a great idea, Liz," Judy said.

"In some years the manager will underperform 12 percent and in some years they will do much better, but I think it is a good solution to your problem, Judy."

"Is the plan locked in?" she asked.

"No. If you need additional money you can sell more units. You can terminate the plan at any time, or you can add more money to it. It is the most flexible, long-term income-generating plan around."

"Someone at work suggested an annuity. Is it similar to a withdrawal plan?" Judy questioned.

"No. With an annuity, your money is locked in at a specific interest rate, and if interest rates are low when you buy it, the contracted monthly payment is low. You can't change your mind once you buy an annuity. You're generally stuck with it. An annuity is not what you need at this point in time. An annuity is a good financial tool if interest rates are high."

"How risky is this withdrawal plan, Liz?" Judy asked.

"It depends on the type of investment plan you choose. A withdrawal plan can be set up through any of the various types of investments a manager offers. The key consideration again should be your age and Judy, if you do not intend to use this money for five years, the fluctuations in the market should work to your advantage over time and you should end up ahead. There will be some years when you will be withdrawing more than the fund earns and other years when it might earn 15 or 20 percent, so it averages out."

"I think this is maybe what I am looking for, but I don't want to eat into my capital," Judy said.

"Okay, here's a 10-year record of a withdrawal plan offered by one of the top managers. Let's see where you would be today, had you invested this money 10 years ago. Now remember as we do this that we are looking back only. There is no way to look forward. If we could, we all would have been multi-millionaires long ago.

"If, in December 1983, you had invested your $200,000 with this particular manager and withdrawn $2,000 each month for 10 years until December 1993, you would have redeemed $240,000 and still have $276,637 left."

"How can that be?" Judy questioned.

"I know it sounds impossible, but it's due to a couple of key factors. One, the power of compounding, that is, reinvesting your income annually and allowing it to grow. Two, the growth in the market. This example is based on an equity fund. A bond fund would not have grown as much, but over the years the volatility would not have been as great, which would only have been important if you wanted to sell. Remember, if the market is down you only have a paper loss, not a real loss unless you actually sell.

"The withdrawal plan is a great investment tool used by widows and widowers, for example, who need additional cash monthly but want to preserve their capital for the children. One of the last investments I helped a client make, just before I retired, was a withdrawal plan. His father had died and left him quite a sum of money. He and his wife were not unlike you and Mark, Annie. They wanted to save the money for the future, but thought some additional cash coming in monthly would help them until they become more established. We opened a withdrawal plan and they are receiving $1,000 a month. They were very pleased to have the added security of the money as well as an additional $12,000 a year. It's a great plan for someone who has a lump sum of money."

"The risk must be great," Annie stated.

"The annual compound rate of return on this particular fund, which is one of the oldest in Canada, is very impressive. One year was 36.3 percent, three years 27 percent, five years 16.5 percent, and ten years 14.9 percent, and this includes 1987, which, as you know, was a disastrous year for the stock market. Fifteen years 16.5 percent, 20 years 18.5 percent and since its inception 39 years ago, 15.6 percent. There are risks, but the risk is minimal with a long-term plan.

"That's why it is so important to clearly define your goals. You must establish your time frame and what you are trying to accomplish. People are always so concerned with risk. They want the highest rate of return possible with a guarantee, but life simply doesn't come with guarantees. If you need the money within a short time period, stay out of the market, but if you are building your future, history shows us that there is no better place for a long-term investment than in the equity market. That is why I keep repeating that one of the keys to investing is the time frame, as age, I believe, is a critical factor. Investors who think they can make a quick buck are not investors, they are gamblers, and they might just as well go to Las Vegas."

"Annie, I've been listening to your concern about risk and it seems to me that it is just as risky not to allow your money to get the most for you. Inflation is the killer." I explained. "We've seen this with the value of homes. In addition to that as you grow in your career and begin to make good money, you just simply adjust your life style. The more you earn, the more you demand, the more you spend. So it is probably as difficult for you today as it was for me a few years ago. It has only been in the past seven or eight years that I started to become serious about my future. It was then that I started to buy Canada Savings Bonds. I only wish that I had started earlier and understood mutual funds, especially with my RRSP.

"My first car was a Volkswagen and I found it expensive. Now I drive a Lexus, and even though I earn five times what I did in the old days, the Lexus is at least five times as expensive as the Volkswagen. My clothes, my home, the restaurants I go to, the vacations I take now, all cost more: the more you earn, the more you spend. Life is one great treadmill."

"I guess it is a question of priorities," said Annie. "You have to make a concerted effort to save. I'm on my way. I now have my first RRSP, thanks to Liz. I don't know yet, how it will affect my tax return, but my money is sitting in a money market account in the RRSP," said Annie.

"Yes, Liz, me too. Bob made a spousal contribution into an RRSP for me this year, so I have some more money to invest. I want to buy some more stock in the computer company," Ruth said emphatically.

"I think we are all sitting with our RRSP contributions ready to go, Liz. I know the Canada Savings Bonds that I put in my plan are not earning what other investments are," I said.

"Alright. What we have to do is take one of you at a time and discuss your options," Liz said, arranging her note pad like a secretary ready to take dictation.

"Let's start with you, Annie. What are you going to do?" Liz asked.

"Well, I want to double my money every three years for the next 35 years." She laughed, along with the rest of us.

"Seriously, I deposited $3,000 and being so young, as you have repeatedly pointed out, I think that I am going to invest in an equity fund, one that is fairly aggressive. Doug supplied me with four different financial statements and prospectuses on different funds. I have read them thoroughly and with his help, I have selected a company that has a good track record. Although the fund I've selected is relatively new, the company has averaged 17 percent for the past three years which is when the fund started. They are investing in small-to medium-sized companies. Doug also pointed out that they own shares in the company that I work for, so I think they are very wise."

"Well, haven't we done our homework!" Ruth teased.

"Yes, I have. I read a report and watched a financial show which explained that the future of the country is in the hands of small-to mid-sized companies, and when I see the growth that my company has had over the past four years, I believe it. So based on this information I have made my selection," Annie asked.

"I think you've made a good choice and understanding that you own part of the company should keep you very interested and productive at work," Liz responded.

"I'm not quite finished. I set up a PAC on a monthly basis and I am going to purchase another fund the company manages. I had to borrow part of this year's contribution and I don't want to be stuck again next year, so Doug is arranging for $250 to come out of my bank account every month on the 15th, which is when I get paid," she continued. "It is really very easy, just a matter of signing a form and providing a blank sample cheque, which he sent to the mutual fund company. Beginning next month they will deduct the money from my bank account, every month, until I advise them otherwise. I am buying a speciality fund that has performed quite well for the last two years. Doug says that when investing on a monthly basis, he suggests looking for a volatile fund like an emerging market fund and buying it over a period of time. He explained that the emerging markets should do well over the next five years and if I can take advantage of their ups and downs, I should do very well. I feel great, and I am very pleased with Doug. He really took his time with me. He explained the manager's investment philosophy and what types of companies he looks for. I really feel like I have accomplished something," Annie said, as she raised her thumb in victory. "I want to thank you Liz. I would never have come this far or felt so confident if it hadn't been for this exercise."

"You are very welcome, Annie. I am so pleased that you have a plan in place, and Doug is right about buying on a monthly basis. Just don't give up on your strategy. If after a few years of buying this fund it makes a good return, you can change your option and buy something else out of favour or declining. It is an excellent approach for a monthly plan.

"All right, one down, four to go," Liz said. "Judy, what are you going to do?"

"I have deposited $4,000 to my RRSP and it is sitting with the rest of my RRSP money at the bank. I am going to transfer it to this company," she said, handing Liz a brochure. "I have chosen this manager because she seems to have an international focus. I have a total of $17,000 in my plan and I want to invest as much outside of Canada as I can. I am working with Doug as well and he agreed that taking an international approach was a good strategy. This company has two unique funds which are 100 percent eligible for RRSPs but they invest all over the world. One is an equity fund and the other a bond fund. I only want $5,000 purely Canadian and I want to make sure that my maximum goes into the emerging markets. I, too, have been following the news and the Canadian dollar is in trouble. I think it's a good idea to get outside of Canada."

"What you are suggesting is a very aggressive portfolio, Judy. Remember, if the Canadian dollar rises you could lose money in the foreign funds with the currency conversion. In addition, the emerging markets have been proven to be quite volatile, with wide swings in the market."

"Yes, I understand, but as you know, I also have a sizeable amount of money which Doug placed into a very conservative withdrawal plan. I shouldn't need to touch my RRSP money until I retire, and 20 years should bring greater stability to the emerging countries. I understand the risk and I'm prepared to take it."

"It sounds as though you have a handle on what you are doing and it appears to be a good approach. If you have no intention of touching the money, I think that you'll do very well," Liz reassured. "Two down. What about our teacher friend with the big pension, Cathy?" Liz teased.

"Quite frankly, I am still apprehensive about the market and I don't think that I am able to make decisions like the rest of you. I'm just not that comfortable," Cathy replied.

"You mean you want to leave your money in a money market account?" Ruth questioned.

"I guess I'm one of those people who want a high rate of return and a guarantee that I'm not going to lose my investment," she responded.

"I can understand that," Liz stated. "Not everyone is comfortable investing in the market and if it is going to keep you awake at night, you are better off staying away. How much were you able to put in your RRSP, Cathy?"

"Well, I am restricted because of my teacher's pension, but I hadn't contributed before so I had a catch-up from previous years. I was able to put in $4,500. I guess the problem I am having is that I took the money from my savings account, where it was safe, and that makes me nervous. I also get like this when I buy a new car. I enjoy looking at my passbook and seeing the money sitting there. It gives me a great sense of security."

"Cathy, here is a suggestion. You'll more than likely receive at least a $1,500 tax refund based on the amount you contributed. Why don't you invest $1,500 in an asset allocation fund, where the manager makes all the decisions, and leave the balance of $3,000 in a nice and safe money market fund? When you get the $1,500 back from the government, put it back into your savings account and build it up again. That way the only money at risk is the $1,500 that you wouldn't have had anyway, if you hadn't made a contribution. Next year, depending on how you feel, you can always change your strategy," Liz offered.

"Yes, that might work. I would really be ahead at that point, wouldn't I. I would still have my $4,500 tucked away in my RRSP and I'd be ahead $1,500 from my tax refund," she replied.

"Who's handling your RRSP?" Liz asked.

"Remember that RRSP seminar we attended last month? I met a financial advisor there who I really feel comfortable with. Actually, she's a former teacher and that's probably one of the reasons that I feel so relaxed with her. She suggested that we move $250 a month from the money market, in the RRSP, to a conservative mutual fund, still in the RRSP, to take advantage of the dollar-cost averaging that you talked to us about. That also would allow me to control the money for a longer timeframe, and if I become uncomfortable, I can stop the transfer at any time."

"That's an excellent approach, one quite frankly that I didn't think about. You could do that with the $1,500 dollars that represents your tax refund and see how you feel after six months. Perfect!" Liz said supportively.

"Wait a minute! I've been so focused on the investment side of my RRSP that I forgot that I'll have a refund this year from Revenue Canada," Annie suddenly remembered. "I'll be able to buy that new colour television that we want for the rec room."

"Or possibly pay off the RRSP loan, Annie?" I said.

"Oh, right. That's what I meant," she frowned. "I forgot about that."

"Don't be sad, you borrowed to save," Ruth said. "I think that's smart, Annie, and I really hope that you continue with your RRSP each and every year until you are ready to retire. Bob has been contributing for 20 years and he has a good-sized RRSP. In two years he'll retire, and had he not been contributing each year without fail, we wouldn't be in as good shape financially as we are. It'll make our retirement years worth all the hard work and hopefully we can spend a good part of them in the sunny south."

"Ruth, you're number four. What are you going to do?" Liz asked.

"Buy some more stock," she replied.

"Don't you think you've taken enough of a chance with your computer stock?" Cathy asked.

"I look at it this way. We seem to have enough money today to retire comfortably, and when I look at Bob's RRSP, which is mainly in very conservative, fixed-income investments, I think that there is room for some risk. Besides, I love it. I find it fascinating following the market, and I'm so excited when my stock goes up. These sessions have really given me something to look forward to. I've almost taken on the stock market as a hobby and it has opened up a whole new world for me. Seven months ago I would gather up the paper in the morning, take out the life section and give the rest to Bob. Now he gets the sports section until I'm finished with the business report. I never thought I would find a new interest at this stage of my life. I guess I have been floundering since the kids all left home. Bob is amazed at my change and we are having more conversations now than we have had in years. I listen to him talk about his work and I'm starting to understand the business. Remember that I've haven't worked since before I was married. So I am going to buy stock," she stated emphatically.

"I guess you have stated your case, but remember that the only stock that you have purchased so far has gone up. It could go down, Ruth. How are you going to feel then?" Liz asked.

"If the fundamentals that made be buy it are still there, I'll wait and if I have made a mistake, I'll sell and cut my losses," she replied.

"I don't believe this," Annie said rolling her eyes. "I thought little old ladies were supposed to knit, Ruth."

"Unfortunately, so did I. Leave me alone Annie, I'm enjoying this new world that I've found myself in."

"So what are you going to buy?" Liz asked.

"I have some questions first. What is a strip coupon?"

"Good question, Ruth. A strip coupon is an excellent investment for an RRSP."

"That's good. Because Bob has some in his plan."

"Some bonds, when they are issued, come with coupons attached which represent the interest portion," Liz explained. "Barb, if you have been buying Canada Savings Bonds for a long time, you'll remember that they were once issued with coupons all coming due at some time in the future."

"No, but I remember my Dad, every November, sitting at the kitchen table cutting coupons."

"That's exactly what a broker does. Not with Canada Savings Bonds but with government and corporate bonds, only they cut them off before they mature. They strip the coupons from the bond and price them individually, based on market conditions, quality of the bond, current interest rates and how long until maturity, then sell each coupon and bond separately."

"You mean by maturity, the date when the coupon is worth its face value?" Ruth asked.

"Yes, if a coupon's face value is $5,000 payable in nine years, the coupon will be priced, for example at $3,700. If interest rates fall, the price of the coupon will rise dramatically. If this happens, it may become a trading vehicle and investors, having earned a good return, will sell. But anyone holding the coupon until maturity will get the face value of $5,000."

"Is that guaranteed?" Ruth asked.

"Yes, provided it is a highly rated issue. Remember, the quality of all these investments depends on the issuer. People who are nearing retirement usually stagger the maturity dates of the coupons they buy, planning for one to come due each year, which provides them with a set amount of income each year."

"That's a good strategy," Ruth said. "Thank's, Liz. I'll tell Bob that he is on the right track."

"I'm sure he'll appreciate your insight," Liz laughed.

"Another question, can I buy a U.S. investment, in my self-directed RRSP? I don't mean just a foreign mutual fund, I mean a company that is listed on the New York Stock Exchange."

"Yes, you can, but remember that it forms part of your 20 percent foreign content," Liz replied.

"We've talked about our investments. Will you tell us what you own, Liz?" Ruth asked. "Or is that too bold a question?"

"No, I don't mind sharing with you my investment strategy, but please remember that I was in the business and had so much information available to me that I changed my portfolio often and quickly. A new report or idea came across my desk every hour, and I still get the reports from my company, so for me it is difficult to be committed to any one investment for very long, and that can be a mistake.

"Right now I own shares in a gold company, an oil company, a mutual fund management company, and a retail company and I also own shares in the same computer company that you own shares in, Ruth. The rest of my investments are in mutual funds. I consider my mutual fund investments the conservative part of my portfolio. My foreign investments are in a telephone company in an emerging country, a far east fund and a European fund."

"You are very diversified," Ruth commented.

"Part of the strategy, remember?" Liz replied.

"Well, Bob made two year's contribution to my spousal plan and he is at the maximum limit, so I have a good start. Please give me the actual names of the companies that you have invested in and I'll have my broker send me the information on those stocks. I'll check them for you, Liz, and ensure that you have good investments."

"Thank you very much, Ruth, I look forward to your analysis," Liz said, as we all laughed at the suggestion of Ruth advising Liz.

"I have also given Bud a list of companies that I am interested in."

"Sounds like a lot of work, Ruth," Cathy said.

"I told you that I have taken this on as a hobby. It keeps me busy."

"How can Bob make two year's contribution when you said he has been contributing every year?" Cathy asked.

"He made last year's and this year's. Apparently you can make a contribution in January or February for both years."

"Most people contribute in February for last year, but by contributing early for next year you have the advantage of sheltering the income. Remember, the three-year spousal rule, Ruth. If Bob is planning to retire in two years you must be careful when you deregister to leave your spousal plan for three years after Bob makes the last contribution."

"No problem. We probably won't touch any of the RRSPs until he turns 71. That's five years away, so we'll be alright."

"What happens at that point?" Annie asked.

"RRSP holders have a few options," Judy explained.

"One, you can deregister, cash out the whole RRSP and pay tax, which is not advisable unless your plan is very small or possibly if you are leaving the country permanently. Two, you can buy an annuity, which must be done with care and timing because once you make a decision, you have to live with it. Or three, which is the most popular, you can transfer your RRSP to a Registered Retirement Income Fund, which is really an extension of the RRSP except that it has a required minimum pay-out each year."

"What if the minimum is not enough to live on?" Annie asked.

"No problem," Judy continued. "You can set your own schedule of payments. But remember, this is money that you have never paid tax on. Now is the time to pay the piper, Revenue Canada. The tax schedule applicable to earned income is applied to the payments received from the plan."

"Well, Barb, we've come to you. You made your contribution with your Canada Savings Bonds, right? Do you have any thoughts about what changes you would like to make to your portfolio?" Liz asked me.

"Yes, I have been thinking about it and really the only investment that I've ever been exposed to is real estate. Given our talk about buying when the prices are down, I can't believe that real estate prices can possibly go any lower, so I would like to look at a real estate investment and mortgages. I was able to make up my carry-forward amount which, with this year's contribution amount, comes to $25,000. I opened my RRSP with a trust company and I was able to designate Ruth's broker, Bud, as my financial advisor, allowing him to trade on my account," I said.

"That's a great start. If you are in the highest tax bracket you should receive a refund of around $13,000," Liz said.

"Yes, and I still have some bonds left, which I could redeem and use the money to invest," I said.

"Well, you know Revenue Canada allows a cushion of $8,000 as an over-contribution to an RRSP."

"What do you mean a 'cushion'?" Annie asked.

"A few years ago, when you made a contribution it was based on that year's income. Now when you make your contribution, it is based on the earnings of the previous taxation year. When you receive your assessment, it states how much you can contribute up to the first 60 days of next year, to reduce this year's tax based on last year's income. Because of this reporting, it is possible, particularly if you belong to a pension plan, that you may overcontribute. In order to protect yourself, you are allowed a cushion of $8,000 for the lifetime of the RRSP to overcontribute without a penalty. If someone like Barb, who doesn't belong to a pension plan, puts in an additional $8,000, she can't deduct it, but the income generated on the $8,000 is tax sheltered, and if you leave it long enough, even though you pay tax on it when you take it out, you have $8,000 generating income and compounding say for 25 years. It can have a considerable effect on your plan."

"So I should consider contributing this additional money," I stated.

"Yes, but I would only do it if you have money that you are not going to use, especially money that is generating taxable interest income. Barb, you are in the highest tax bracket, which means that for every dollar you receive in income, you pay approximately 50¢ in the form of tax to the government."

"How did we ever get into this mess? Somehow it isn't right that so much of our earnings goes to taxes," Judy said.

"We live in a large country which is used to and demands the best social services. The problem is that we don't have enough people to support such a heavy burden. There's not much that we can do about it," Cathy explained.

"No, I guess not. I certainly don't want to decrease my day-to-day comfort level in order to cut taxes," I said. "If I contributed the additional $8,000, it would give me enough money to hold a mortgage in my RRSP. If anyone needs a mortgage let me know," I said.

"That's a generous offer, Barb. Can she do that Liz?" Ruth asked.

"Yes, a mortgage qualifies as an RRSP investment. Many people hold mortgages in their RRSPs, and there are very few restrictions. You can set your own rate of interest and payment schedule, which can be very flexible, provided it is an arm's-length transaction," Judy explained.

"Hold it. What is this arm's-length thing?" Annie asked.

"It means that you are not dealing with yourself or an immediate relative," I explained. "If you are, you are said to be dealing at non-arm's-length."

"That's right," Liz agreed.

"You mean that I could hold my own mortgage in my RRSP?" Annie asked.

"Yes, but there are very strict rules that apply to holding your own mortgage in your plan, and it can be very expensive," Judy said.

"Why would it be more expensive than if you held a stranger's mortgage?" Annie asked with keen interest.

"The rule says that you can't derive a benefit from your RRSP and Revenue Canada views this personal mortgage transaction as just that, so in order to prevent abuse, they insist that the mortgage be insured, which can cost up to two percent of the mortgage amount. There also must be a certified appraisal and the mortgage must be administered by an approved lender. The interest rate charged must be approximately the same as the lender's current interest rate. All of these features or rules add additional costs. Very few people use this option, as they find that once all of the costs have been accounted for, it isn't worth it," Judy said.

"It sounds like a good idea," Annie says. "I don't understand why you have to insure your own mortgage. If you die, who cares anyway?"

"The insurance is not life insurance, Annie, it is default insurance," Judy explained. "If you didn't make your payments on your mortgage in your RRSP, the administrator would advise the insurance company that you are in arrears and they could take steps to evict you and sell your house. If the selling price didn't cover the mortgage, the insurer would have to make up the difference to your RRSP."

"You mean, if I defaulted on my own RRSP mortgage, the insurer could put me out of my own house. I can't believe it," Annie stammered.

"Your RRSP is treated separately from you personally and even though it is your money, under trust law it is a separate entity," Judy clarified.

"Should I look at a real estate fund, Liz?" I asked.

"Yes you can, or alternatively, I know of nothing that would prevent you from holding a mortgage or several small ones for some of your real estate clients, Barb," Liz replied. "There is no question that if there was ever a time to buy a real estate fund, it is probably now. The prices are very low. I guess the question is, will they recover and if they do, when?"

"I've been in this business for many years and I have yet to see the market not recover. People have to live somewhere," I replied.

"Remember that most real estate funds invest in commercial real estate, which has been devastated in some parts of the country, and it may take a long time for the market to absorb all of the properties developed during the late '80s and early '90s. So if that is your choice, take a long-term view of it."

"Well, I don't have to put it all into a real estate fund. I think that I'll put in only $10,000 and I'll also put $5,000 into the same fund that Annie chose, the Canadian growth fund. Should I leave the rest in the Canada Savings Bonds until I find someone who wants a small mortgage?" I asked.

"You can. The Bank of Canada does not drop the interest rate once they have set it, however they can and do raise it periodically when interest rates are rising. They are redeemable at any time, but you should cash them on the first of the month," Liz stated.

"Why on the first of the month?" Cathy asked.

"You'll not receive any more interest on the 20th than you would on the first of the same month, so always cash your bonds on the first of the month.

"I guess that takes care of our investments. I think that you are all on the right track. The markets are down and it's a good time to buy. I am confident that you now have enough knowledge to implement your plans and I believe that you have chosen good investments.

"Once you receive confirmations of your investments, I'll show you how to read them and how to follow your investments in the paper," Liz said.

"Yes, we can take them to Florida," Annie reminded her, looking towards Barb.

"Yes, if you want to go, let me know no later than the end of next week and I'll make all the reservations for you. A friend of mine owns a travel agency and he can co-ordinate it for us," I said.

"Oh," said Annie. "A male friend, Barb?"

"You are so bold, Annie," Ruth said.

"Yes, Annie, a male friend. He owns the whole building and he and his wife of 35 years are going to stay in their unit on the next floor," I said.

"Alright," she said, disappointed.

"But he does have a single brother," I replied.

Her eyes sparkled as if she had just discovered the biggest secret in the world and only she knew it.

"See you in Florida." Annie waved as she headed out the door.

Chapter Eight
April

Everyone was so excited when they emerged from the airport. The plane had been late and I had waited at least an hour for them to clear customs.

"Oh, feel the heat, look at the trees, everything is so green," Cathy rejoiced in the sunlight. "I can't believe that I haven't done this before."

Annie actually dropped to her knees on the grass just outside the terminal exit doors.

"Oh, I'm in heaven, thank you, God," she sang.

"Did you arrange for the car, Barb?" Ruth asked, dragging Annie up from the ground.

"Yes, I did, a convertible, just as you asked," I replied. Ruth had insisted that the car be rented in her name. Unknown to the rest of us, when Annie's mother couldn't rent a car in Arizona, Ruth had panicked. She didn't have a credit card, either. She told me that, the day after that second meeting, she had arranged through her bank to have one issued in her name. This was the first time she had used it and the car rental was to be her treat.

We hadn't been at the condo for 15 minutes when all of us, after slipping into our bathing suits, grabbed a cool drink and headed for the pool.

No one said a word for the first half hour, as we absorbed the afternoon sun. Even Cathy, who was so terrified of being exposed to the sun, stretched out on the lounger, her ever-faithful straw hat covering her face. Finally Judy spoke.

"Well, what are the plans?" she asked.

"I don't care if I move from this spot for the whole week," Liz said. "This is as close to perfect as life can get."

"I think Canada should buy a tropical island," Annie piped up. "Think of all the money the government could earn from the tourists. No country needs a tropical island more than Canada."

"Maybe the government could continue to finance the Old Age Pension Plan from the profits," Ruth responded.

"Yes, that reminds me, no matter what we do this week, we must take one afternoon and focus on our meeting. After all, that's what started this in the first place," I said.

"Somebody should get a newspaper and find out if it is going to rain. We'll hold our meeting then," Annie said.

"I hope you all brought at least one fairly dressy outfit," I said. "I have arranged for dinner tonight at one of the best restaurants in the area. My accountant called yesterday and informed me that I have a large refund coming back on my income tax. I couldn't believe it! I have always had to pay in the past, but it was because of the large RRSP contribution I made. So dinner is on me."

"That's great!" Liz said. "That's what's so nice about the RRSP contribution - you see the effects of it quickly. I am really pleased for you, Barb."

"We owe a lot to you, Liz. I think that all of us feel much better about life after accomplishing so much this winter," I said.

"Oh, please, don't mention winter, you just sent a chill right down my spine," Annie said. "She is right though, Liz. Thank you so much for all that you've done for us."

"Well, I only guided you and it was my pleasure. You have only yourselves to thank, because you took action."

"Who would have thought last year, when we started this, that we would all be sitting here in the sunny south, with our investment plans in place, enjoying the life of the rich and famous," Annie said, dreamily.

"Well, not quite, but we are on our way," Judy stated.

"I feel so guilty," Ruth said.

"No guilt allowed on this trip," Judy said.

"I can't help it. I have a dear friend, an old school chum actually, who I have stayed in touch with since grade school, if you can imagine. Anyway, she lost her husband three years ago and she is really struggling. I spoke to her last week and she is investigating something called a reverse mortgage on her house. I told her that I didn't know anything about it, but I said that I would ask Liz or Judy this week. I didn't have the heart to tell her that I was jaunting off to Florida on vacation," Ruth said.

"What is a reverse mortgage?" Cathy asked, through the brim of her hat.

"Just what the name suggests - instead of you making mortgage payments, an insurance company pays you. There is a lot of controversy about this product," Judy replied.

"What is its purpose?" Ruth asked.

"Unfortunately, a lot of people find themselves short of cash when they retire, yet their home, which is generally an individual's largest asset, is free and clear. A reverse mortgage allows homeowners to take equity out of their house without having to make mortgage payments. They can receive a combination of a lump sum of money and a monthly income. The monthly income is generated through an annuity which is purchased. An insurance company advances the money after registering a mortgage against the property. No payments are made on the mortgage and the unpaid interest accumulates and the debt grows until the death of the owners or the sale of the home.

"Older people don't like to be forced to leave their homes and this concept allows them to stay in it while giving them the cash flow required to keep them going."

"Gee, that sounds like a good idea to me," Annie said. "My mother could have used this if they hadn't sold the house. What is the controversy?"

"Number one, you are only entitled to a certain percentage of the value of the home. Let's say that your home is worth

$250,000. The insurance company may give you only $80,000. Number two, for all of you who currently have a mortgage and look at your statement every year, you will recognize how little the principal amount is reduced after making a year's payment."

"Boy, this is certainly true. Our payment is $1,200 a month and most of that is interest," Annie stated.

"With a reverse mortgage, the interest compounds and is added to the mortgage, and over say 20 years, it is entirely possible that all or most of the equity in your home will be gone, because of interest owed on the mortgage. A reverse mortgage is really no different than a regular mortgage, except that you don't make payments."

"So it is possible that the outstanding interest could eat into the equity and if you sold the home there may not be anything left," Ruth said.

"That is a possibility but the appreciation in the value of the home should offset the growing interest amount. I think that this product is probably best used by someone fairly senior in years, with little or no income and who has no survivors to whom they wish to leave their estate."

"That is precisely the situation my friend is in. She never had any children, and she certainly doesn't want to move out of her house," Ruth explained.

"She is probably the proper candidate, but she may be too young, Ruth. Another alternative for her is to sell her home, invest the money and move to a seniors' complex or rent an apartment. But her investment income would then be taxable, and she would have the expense of renting," Judy said. "She should maybe look into selling her home and putting her money in a withdrawal plan, like I did."

"Ruth," Liz broke in, "she should seek a second opinion. A reverse mortgage is an extreme solution to a critical problem. She should review her situation very closely. Most people who want to stay in their homes in their senior years have such an emotional attachment to them, yet it is beyond their ability to care for them. The house is probably much larger than she needs and the yard work may become a burden and the stairs too difficult to manage. If, while she is still active, she makes the choice on her own to relocate to a smaller, more efficient apartment, she is then not locked into an agreement where the equity in her home is being eaten up by interest payments. She, at some point, will have to leave the house and may have nothing left."

"You know, you are so right, Liz," Ruth agreed. "Even Bob and I are talking about moving into a condominium after he retires. We've had a house most of our married life and it would be nice to wake up on Saturday morning and listen to someone else cutting the lawn."

"Each situation has to be examined very carefully. This is not just a financial decision, it is a lifestyle decision and I think your friend should not be too quick with her decision. She should take the time to explore her options. If after she has done so, she then decides that the reverse mortgage is the solution, then she should by all means go ahead. Many people have done it."

"Thanks, I'll tell her. Would anybody like another drink?" Ruth asked, as she rose from her lounge chair.

"Look at the time! It is 4:30, there are only two bathrooms, ladies, and six of us to get ready for dinner by 6:00. Besides, you have had too much sun already. I vote for heading in," I said.

"Yes, let's go," Cathy said.

Dinner was excellent, and the relaxed atmosphere set the tone for the balance of the vacation. Just being able to walk outside without our winter gear was in itself a pleasure. And the prices! Dinner for six cost the same as lunch for three in Canada. The rest of the week was spent in pure pleasure, shopping, sightseeing, swimming, relaxing around the pool, walking on the beach, all the while eating the best seafood available. It was glorious.

Annie called home three or four times during the week to check on Brett and we always had a good laugh after the call, as she recounted the problems and minor crises that Mark had related to her. Brett had apparently redecorated his room with the help of a black marker, and Mark was busy painting the room before Annie returned home. Bob called twice, looking for things only Ruth knew how to find, and that thrilled us as well. Cal never called. Cathy explained that he was an excellent cook - she confessed that he was a better cook than she was. He had also arranged to go to two ball games while she was away, so she would hardly be missed.

Finally, the end of our vacation drew near.

"Listen, it is Friday, and we are scheduled to go home tomorrow," Liz said, "Let's sit down today and have our session, but I insist that we do it by the pool."

Loaded down with suntan lotion, towels, books and sunglasses, we headed out for their last afternoon in the sun. With tropical drinks filled with ice, we relaxed as we began our April session.

Throughout the week, Ruth had been buying the *Wall Street Journal*, studying the markets and generally keeping up with current events. Liz had called her friends back at the office a few times to check on market conditions.

"Ruth, I think that you should update us on what has been happening over the past week, while we have been letting the world go by," Judy suggested.

"The markets have been acting wildly, the U.S. raised the interest rate again, and there is a crisis in the Middle East which is making everybody nervous," she related. "All of the U.S markets are down."

"What will all of this do to our investments, Liz?" Annie asked.

"The markets in Canada are down as well. Our interest rates are up, as we are generally forced to raise ours when the U.S. does," she replied.

"Why is that? Can't we stand on our own two feet?" Annie asked.

"No, we can't. I told you a while ago that Canada is so closely tied to the U.S. that their every move affects us. Especially interest rates. If our rate falls below the U.S. rate, foreign investors will move their money out of Canada to the U.S. and the value of our dollar will fall. If our dollar falls, it'll speed up the exit of the remaining investment dollars in Canada. Its like a slinky going down the stairs, the further it goes, the faster it does it."

"Why does this happen?" Cathy asked.

"People become concerned that the market will fall more, so they sell their stock, and if interest rates are high they'll move some of their money back to the safer investments," Liz responded. "The equity markets are driven by emotion, which makes them so unpredictable."

"Should we be concerned and move our money out of the market, Liz?" Judy asked.

"No, you are in for the long term and you'll experience many a downward movement. Remember that the markets never move in a straight line. You have to learn to be patient and take advantage of a downward trend," Liz stated.

"How do we do that?" Annie asked.

"You have already started, Annie. If the market keeps going down every month that you buy your mutual fund in your RRSP, you'll be buying cheaper shares," Liz said. "This is called dollar cost averaging, remember? Buying an investment on a monthly plan is the best way to take advantage of all market conditions."

"Yes, I did the same. Last month I opted to transfer $250 a month from the money market fund to an equity plan and I'm glad that I did, because I am now buying my shares at a lower price every month," Cathy said. "Can we buy an investment fund using a PAC outside of our RRSP? You know, just like a savings plan?"

"Certainly, you can," Liz responded. "For women who don't have a large sum of money to invest initially, this is a great way to start an investment program. In fact a PAC can be a woman's best financial friend."

"Can you dollar cost average with stocks?" Annie asked.

"Well, you could, except it can become cumbersome and expensive. The minimum number of shares that you should buy is 100, which is referred to as a board lot. You should always buy in even lots. It is difficult to buy a specific dollar amount on a monthly basis. What investors can do is buy more shares at a lower price than what they originally paid. This is called averaging down. The total cost of all of the shares divided by the number of shares will give you a lower per share price."

"That's a good idea. If my computer stock drops, say, to $4 and I buy another 1,000 shares, my price per share drops to $4.50 because I paid $5 for the first 1,000 shares," Ruth reasoned.

"That's right."

"Why should you always buy in even lots, Liz?" Cathy asked.

"Shares are generally bought and sold in multiples of 100s and it is harder to sell an odd number of shares. The broker will also charge a higher commission on an odd lot and the price per share may be lower," Liz explained.

"I was reading the U.S. mutual fund listings and I can't believe how many mutual funds there are in the U.S. It must be difficult for Americans trying to make a decision about what to buy from which company," Ruth commented.

"Yes, the U.S. market is much larger that the Canadian market. That's why it is important to have an investment advisor," Liz said. "The market in Canada is growing as well, and requires full-time attention just to keep up with all of the managers and the different products that they have available."

"Speaking of investment advisors, now that we all have one, what should we expect from them, Liz?" Cathy questioned.

"First of all, they should be calling you more often than you are calling them. They should monitor the investments that you have to ensure that you are still on track with your original plan and that your chosen investments are performing in the manner that they should be. They should be bringing new ideas, new products and other investments to your attention throughout the year and should certainly make sure that your RRSP contribution is made each year. They should send you articles that they think are relevant and any research material or updates from companies. Many advisors may even provide you with a newsletter which some of their firms produce, in addition to the annual reports and updated material that fund managers will send you directly. An investment in a mutual fund requires less attention than an individual stock. Ruth and Barb will probably be talking to their broker about their stock acquisitions much more often than the rest of you will be talking to your advisors about your mutual funds. Any problem or question that you have should encourage you to pick up the telephone and call them."

"I have a question, Liz," Ruth said. "How can an investor possibly know the right thing to do at the right time? I've been reading the market comments this past week and I can't believe how varied the opinions are. No one agrees with anyone else. It is very confusing."

"Ruth, someone said years ago, 'If all of the economists were laid end to end, they'd still point in different directions.' This is so true. No one can predict with any degree of accuracy what will happen tomorrow," Liz explained. "The analysts are giving you their perspective based on their individual analysis and all you can do is read and learn. What they are providing is an educated guess, given the information and historical data that is available."

"But there seems to be very little agreement," Ruth continued with her observations. "Everyone has a different view on which way the market will go and a different reason for why they think it will happen. Just listen to this one page in today's paper: 'The economy will slow down, more than expected. Earnings will be disappointing. The stock market will decline'. That's one report. The very next one says, 'although it will hardly be smooth sailing for the stock market in the near future, we still think that we are in the middle of an intermediate-term up trend'. Still another says, 'this is the best buying opportunity for the past 24 months. I am a buyer'. How is someone supposed to make a decision based on this information?"

"This is why you need to be a long-term investor. No one can predict what is going to happen, and if your investment horizon is greater than three to five years, it simply doesn't matter. Most analysts take a short-term view of market conditions. I suggest that you continue to read, but don't panic. Whatever position you are in today, you'll not necessarily be in the same position tomorrow," Liz replied.

"Which reminds me, Bob is in the process of gathering together the paperwork to do our income tax while I'm away. I hate this time of year," Ruth stated. "He becomes unbearable. Anyway, I took a look at last year's return and noticed that he had a lot of dividend income. Is that a good idea, Liz?"

"Yes," Liz said. "There are three different types of investment income-interest income, dividend income and capital-gains and they are all taxed at different levels. A properly structured portfolio should have a percentage of all types of investments. Interest income is the kind received from a Canada Savings Bond, savings account or a GIC. The government encourages invest-ments in shares of companies as it helps stimulate the market, and in order to accomplish this, the structure of the tax schedule favours equity investments which for the most part generate capital gains.

"Dividend income also has a favourable tax treatment be-cause when a company pays a dividend to the shareholders, it has already paid tax on the money. Dividends are received from stocks or mutual funds.

"There is also a provision for losses in the income tax act, whereby one can deduct capital losses from capital gains."

"You mean that, if the price of my computer stock rises from $5 to $10, but another stock I own falls from $7 to $3, I can deduct my loss from my gain?" Ruth asked.

"Yes, but only when you sell *both* stocks. Every year when you prepare your income tax you list your losses and carry forward that amount to the next year if there is no gain during that year. When you sell a stock in which you have made a profit, you deduct the loss from your gain."

"That seems fair," Annie stated.

"Liz, if capital gains on stock and mutual funds have a favourable tax treatment shouldn't we be holding our equity investments outside the RRSP?" Ruth asked.

"If you only have two investments, one an equity and the other an interest-generating vehicle and you are determined to hold only them, then yes, the equity investment should be outside the plan and the interest-generating investment inside the RRSP,"

Liz confirmed. "But your RRSP goal should be growth. You should never plan your strategy only to accommodate the tax implications. If, as in a long-term plan, I have the opportunity to increase my RRSP to six or seven times its value over 20 or 25 years, why would I settle for a two or three times growth by investing in lower-interest-paying vehicles?"

"I think that is a valid point," Cathy said, "Is there an easy way for us to calculate the approximate amount of money that we'll need to retire on?"

"Yes, I was reading a financial planning article the other day," Judy said, "and they offered to provide you with a future projection. If you tell them how much money per year that you think you'll need to retire on, they will tell you how much capital you'll need to generate that income."

"I can't possibly tell you how much I'll need in 30 years as I can't predict what I'll require," Annie said. "I want to have millions, but I recognise that is unrealistic. I'll retire on what I have been able to save, invest and generate through a RRSP."

"If you tell the financial planner what your current income is, they will determine how much money you'll need to generate enough income to maintain your current lifestyle when you retire," Liz explained. "Financial planners are able to provide you with an amount that factors in inflation."

"Why can't we use the Rule of 72?" Annie asked.

"That's right, at 10 percent it would take approximately 21.5 years to double your money three times," Cathy said, as she made calculations on a piece of paper. "If someone had $50,000 at age

35 they could double it to $100,000 in the first 7 years, $100,000 to $200,000 the second 7 years and $200,000 to $400,000 the last 7."

"But that doesn't tell you how much $400,000 will buy you in 21 years. Inflation is our biggest enemy."

"But Liz," Judy said, "if the withdrawal plan sample that you gave me for $200,000 were $400,000, I could withdraw twice as much, giving me a $48,000 annual income without touching the initial amount. All from a $50,000 investment for 21 years. I can retire on $48,000 a year."

"You can today, because you know what $48,000 will buy. Twenty years ago you could buy three loaves of bread for $1, today one loaf of bread cost $1. That means that your $48,000 would be worth one third or $16,000 in today's dollars."

"Or said another way, we would need 1.2 million dollars, which is three times $400,000, to generate enough money in the future to live at today's $48,000 level," Cathy calculated.

"Exactly!" Liz said.

"Now I'm depressed. I'll never save 1.2 million dollars, even if I live to be 100," Annie protested.

"Here is the bright side. In the early '70s the TSE Index was around 850, approximately one fifth of what it is today," Liz stated.

"So what you are saying is that as long as we are invested in the equity market, our money should grow at a greater rate than inflation," Annie said trying to confirm Liz's statement.

"Yes, that is exactly what I am saying," Liz replied, comforting them.

"I also see, Liz, why you say that time is so important," Annie said.

"Speaking of time, Bob has a number of GIC investments coming due this year and he wants to keep this particular money in GICs, but he will never receive 10 percent interest now. What should he do?"

"There is only one thing to do, Ruth, stagger the maturities. Don't reinvest all of them for the same length of time," Liz suggested.

"You mean invest them to come due in different years, like the strip coupons!" Ruth exclaimed. "Why didn't I think of that, of course."

"Yes, I would add up all the money, divide by five and spread the money over five years, making one come due each year. That way you won't be making wrong timing decisions."

"That's a great idea. You are just so full of knowledge, Liz. Will we ever get to the point where these strategies will come naturally to us?" Ruth asked.

"Yes, you will. You are already on your way. You only have to do something once and you won't forget it. That's what this is all about, knowledge and experience," Liz said, supportively.

"I just remembered something that I had actually forgotten because it has been so long since I've applied for a loan. The mortgage manager at my company reminded me when I talk to him about buying the house before I decided on the withdrawal plan," Judy said. "When you apply for a mortgage and the lender calculates whether or not you can afford the payments, some take into consideration your credit cards, even if you owe nothing on them."

"How can they do that?" Annie asked.

"The bank explained that the fact that you have the credit card entitles you to charge. So they do their calculation based on your credit card limit, take five percent of the total potential debt, as though you were making that payment every month, and include it in your debt column."

"I never heard of such a thing," Annie said.

"Yes, so if you have a credit card with nothing owing but your limit is $5,000, they include five percent or $250 monthly as though it were an actual debt," Judy explained.

"So someone with a large credit limit may not qualify for a loan, even though they owe nothing on their account," Ruth stated.

"That's right," Judy said.

"I guess that when you charge and your repayment schedule is satisfactory and they automatically raise your limit, instead of being proud that they think so much of you, you should decline the offer," Liz suggested.

"Talking about debt. A women that I work with who is in her late 20s received a salary garnishee notice at work," Annie said. "Apparently when she was living at home with her dad, they bought two investment properties together, but they put them in her name to keep the assets away from his second wife. The mortgages were also taken out in my friend's name and when the real estate market turned down and her dad couldn't rent the houses, he defaulted on the payments. The bank sent notice after notice to her father and he ignored them. The houses were then repossessed and sold for $70,000 less than what the mortgages were worth. Because the mortgages are in my friend's name, she now owes the bank the $70,000."

"Oh my, how terrible!" Ruth said. "She must have signed papers. Didn't she realize the risk?"

"I suspect that she didn't consider the risk. The concept of making money on the appreciation of the property was more enticing than the fear of losing," Liz said.

"She must have received legal advice," Cathy said.

"Of course she did, but she was of legal age and should have known what she was getting herself into," Judy said.

"I don't think she should let the lawyer off that easily. But you are right we must be very careful when we sign documents that bind us to a contract that can ultimately come back to haunt us," Liz cautioned. "I wonder, Annie, if your mother would have signed away her right to a spousal pension if she had realized that she could end up with nothing."

"You know, I can't answer that. My dad was a very dominating, strong willed person and I really think that my mother, even if she understood, would still have signed. He probably would have convinced her that he would outlive her."

"I just bought this book yesterday, called *Money and the*

Mature woman, written by Frances Leonard," Ruth said, holding the book for all of us to see. "She makes some interesting points. Listen to what she says. 'In America, more than four out of five wives outlive their husbands. Widows outnumber widowers six to one. Eighty-five percent of women die single but 85 percent of men die married and a typical woman of 65 has 33 percent more life left than a 65 year old man.'"

"So, here we are," Cathy said. "In most cases, men control the money, make all the arrangements and decisions, do the future planning and then die. Women outlive men and we have to live with the plans instituted by them."

"Yes. That's as I see it, but in most cases, it is our own fault," Liz suggested. "The mother of a girlfriend of mine died recently and I was speaking to her dad just two weeks ago. He was asking me investment questions and told me that he was glad that he had survived his wife, because she knew absolutely nothing about money or investing. She never paid a bill. It wasn't his fault that she had no interest or desire to become involved. We can be our own worst enemy."

"What'll your friend at work do, Annie, about the money that she owes?" Cathy asked.

"She'll have to file for bankruptcy."

"What a tragedy. I'll bet that she'll never again sign another document without knowing all about it," Annie said.

"We really have to get our act together. We've come a long way, but situations like this make me think that we have a long way to go," I piped in.

"I was cleaning out a pile of books last month to send to the hospital and I came across an old medical book which started out talking about marriage. The author, a well known male doctor, provided a list of questions a woman should ask herself before getting married, including whether she enjoyed cooking, cleaning and sewing."

"How old was this book?" Annie asked.

"It was published in 1966."

"He probably started the women's movement," Annie suggested.

We all laughed.

"What are you laughing about? We have to start arranging the barbeque for June, so maybe things haven't changed all that much," Judy said.

"Good point, Judy," I said, "But I think things have changed. We arrange the barbeque, but remember the men are in charge of cooking the meat."

"But we still have to clean up!" Cathy snapped.

"I think today, it is more or less a joint effort," I said.

"You're right, Barb," Annie said. "Look at me, I can't possibly imagine my mother leaving my father to care for me while she flew away for a week's vacation, as I just did."

"I agree," I said.

"I think the younger generation has a handle on life, for the most part, much better than mine did. I was never interested in the financial aspect of my life, as Annie is, at her age," Ruth said.

"Speaking about financial knowledge, Liz, I have the newspaper here and it reports that the Dow Jones Industrial Average dropped 10 points yesterday and the bond market was off by 15 basis points," Ruth read. "What is a basis point?"

"A basis point is a convenient way of measuring percentage. When referring to the bond market, a basis point is .01 percent."

"Isn't that what a penny is?" Anne asked.

"Exactly, it is terminology used in the industry to relate to the market movement. For example, if a yield moves from 8 percent to 8.15 percent it means that the yield has increased by 15 basis points. Boy, you guys are starting to get technical."

"You haven't seen anything yet, I would like to take my education further. What investment courses are available to the public?" Ruth asked.

"Back in October we talked about the Canadian Shareowners Association which you can join. They teach you how to pick stocks. In addition to that, you can take a course offered by The Investment Funds Institute of Canada, which educates the representatives selling mutual funds. This is the one that they must take to become licensed, and once you have taken it, you can complete a six-series course in financial planning offered by The Canadian Institute of Financial Planning. This covers Personal Financial Planning, Financial Economics, Taxation, Financial Management, Law and Financial Planning and Advanced Financial Planning. You might check with the local community college; they may offer this program. Or you could take the securities course which the stock brokers must have in order to sell securities. It is offered through The Canadian Securities Institute," Liz replied.

"And these are available to the public? You mean anybody can take them?" Ruth asked.

"Yes, it'll cost you money, of course, but not very much and if you are interested, it is an excellent way to educate yourself. Ruth, with your keen desire to know everything, I would recommend that you do so."

"Next we'll see Ruth going out the door, like me, briefcase in hand heading for Bay Street at 7:30 in the morning," Annie said.

"I don't think so," Ruth replied. "I'm too old to get that involved, but I would like to know more."

"Well, that is one way, a good way," Liz confirmed.

"It is dinner time again," I said, "and you have to pack up to leave tomorrow, so I think we had better get a move on."

"I don't want to go," Cathy said. "This has been a glorious week and just the thought of returning to the winter weather is enough to depress me."

"It'll take me all evening just to cram all of my purchases into my suitcase," Annie groaned. "I may be forced to run out and buy a new bag just to get the stuff home."

"I've done that before. Now I travel with one of those great expandable bags," Liz said.

"Problems, problems, life has really dealt you a hard hand," I said. "I have had a great time, and I'm really sorry that you are leaving me here for another week in this insufferable place."

"Oh, that's right, Barb" Cathy said. "You have another seven days around this dreadful pool. Poor you!"

"Maybe that's when her friend's brother comes on the scene, after we leave. I've been waiting all week for a sign of him," Annie teased.

"Actually, I drop you off at the airport for your flight at 2:00 and he comes in at 2:45."

"Oh, I hope our plane is late I want to meet him," Annie said teasingly. "We want a full report when you get home, Barb."

Chapter Nine
May

In May, the weather finally broke and Canada started to warm up. April showers arrived a month late, frustrating those of us who had waited so patiently for the good weather. But at least the temperature was heading in the right direction.

"It was such a shock to get off the plane and return to the snow last month," Judy said. "I've had a cold since we landed."

We were gathered at Judy's house, which was wall-to-wall planting boxes, all sprouting new life.

"It looks like a greenhouse in here, I've never seen so many different kinds of plants before," Ruth commented.

"I thought that since I am going to be alone this summer, it's a good opportunity to focus on my flower garden."

"You'll certainly be busy," Ruth commented, as she inspected the planting boxes, which were neatly placed close to the windows to take advantage of every bit of sunlight available.

"We had a great trip, Barb. I hope that you can get the condo next year and we get the opportunity to go down again. My skin is still peeling from the sun, but I would do it all over again," Annie said, rubbing her leg.

"Yes, it was wonderful, but I don't know about going there again next year," Ruth said.

"What do you mean, Ruth? Don't you think we would be welcomed back?" Annie questioned. "You would invite us again wouldn't you, Barb?"

"Of course you're welcome," I said, knowing full well what Ruth was hinting at.

"Why would you say that, Ruth, or is it that you wouldn't go back?" Annie queried.

"I think that Barb will be too busy next year to play hostess," she replied, pretending to still be inspecting Judy's plants.

"Ruth probably thinks that I'll be preoccupied next year," I teased.

"Why are you going to be too preoccupied?" Annie asked.

"I'll be getting used to being married," I announced.

Stunned silence. No one spoke for what seemed to be five minutes.

"I can't believe it!" Annie finally stammered. "We didn't even know you had a boyfriend." And then, like a lightening bolt it hit her. "The brother, the brother, you know the friend in Florida's brother," she said waving her arms around wildly.

They all looked at me.

"Is that who it is, Barb?" Judy asked.

"Yes, as Ruth knows, we have been dating on and off for about two years and after you left Florida, he joined me and proposed and I accepted. But I want you to know that I would never let my marriage interfere with our trip next year, if you want to go again."

"This is so exciting," Cathy said. "When is the special day?"

"We haven't set a date yet. Probably sometime in early September," I speculated.

"That's wonderful," Annie said still in shock. "It'll give us time to organize a shower."

"This is a big step for you, Barb," Judy said, "after all these years of being alone. He must be something special."

"Yes, he is special. And yes, it is a big step, one I quite frankly never thought that I would take. But I finally decided that I don't want to spend my remaining years alone. I want to travel and he is a great companion. He is well-established in his business, as I am in mine, and they are both running well enough that we can take some time off and see the world."

"Are you going to live in your house?" Cathy inquired.

"I'm not sure yet. I think that we'll probably sell my house and move to his condo. We have a lot of issues to deal with and we are in the process of signing a pre-nuptial agreement."

"Why do you need a pre-nuptial agreement?" Cathy asked.

"Simply to protect our individual assets. He has children and grandchildren - he's a widower. I certainly don't need anything financial from him and his children should be entitled to his estate when he dies or if something should happen to us. If you don't have an agreement, financial matters can get pretty messy if something happens."

"Yes, I worried the about my assets the whole time Paul was living with me, as we didn't have an agreement. I had all of the assets and he had all the debt. But don't you think signing a contract takes the romance out of the planning?" Judy asked.

"Some people may think so, but anyone who has been married and divorced or widowed should understand the common sense of it," I suggested.

"I suppose that remarrying or marrying later in life comes with a whole new set of rules. When you are young there aren't enough assets to worry about," Ruth said.

"That's right. We want to protect what assets have already been accumulated, but we have a clause that states that we share in any business venture we may create together in the future and if we were to divorce, support payments would only be subject to our financial situation at the time," I explained.

"That's a good idea, but is this document enforceable in court?" Judy asked.

"It is my understanding that it is, provided all our assets have been disclosed when we sign it and we understand the consequences of the contract. I don't think there'll be a problem. It would be difficult to establish that two business people didn't understand a document we both helped prepare."

"And what about your estate?" Ruth asked.

"If I were to survive him, I would get the matrimonial home and his children would be the beneficiaries of the rest of his estate. The same applies to him regarding the home and my estate will go to whomever I designate."

"I think that you are smart, Barb," Liz said. "My sister lived with a fellow for five years and when they split up, she lost most of her furniture, a car that she had bought and half her home. She had a good income and the court awarded him support for two years until he got a job."

"You mean he didn't work and she had to pay him alimony? I can't believe it! Times certainly have changed," Ruth said.

"It isn't that he didn't want to work. He was a victim of a large company cutback and he was 49 years old. It took him all that time to find another job."

"You just don't know what the future will bring, do you?" Judy said.

"May I assume that we are all invited to the wedding, Barb?" Annie asked.

"Yes, it'll be small wedding. I would like each of you there."

"I want to buy you an expensive gift, but my stock has taken such a tumble that I'll probably be destitute by September," Ruth said, playfully.

"I told you, you were taking too great a risk," Annie said flippantly.

"The fundamentals of the company haven't changed, Ruth, and if you have more money, I would suggest that you buy more shares and average down your price," suggested Liz.

"That is a bold move, Liz, but I'm afraid to buy more. What if I lose it all?"

"The company is not going to go out of business. Just the other night on TV they were interviewing the president of a large corporation and he explained how many shares in the company he had and what his net worth was. He has a paper loss of over a million dollars in this downturn but he said that his stock price has declined and recovered four times in the past seven years. The company is still in business, doing well and the stock will come back."

"This is a risky business, isn't it, Liz," Judy said. "I looked at the prices of my mutual funds as well and I'm down. Should I move to another investment?"

"We are in this for the long term and none of you need the money today, so please stop checking the newspaper every day until this market turns around, and trust me, it will.

"Each one of you, with the exception of Judy, owns a home and in the past four years you have lost at least 15 percent of the value of your home because of declining real estate prices, yet not one of you would consider selling your house because you have lost money and afraid of losing more. If you were going to sell, you would wait until the prices climbed back, unless for some reason you needed to sell. None of you are in a position of having to sell your investments. Stay calm."

"You are right, but it is just unnerving to see your investment decline a little everyday. I feel rather helpless," Ruth said.

"I was the nervous one," Cathy said, "but because prices have declined so much over the past few months, I just moved half of my money from the money market fund and bought an equity mutual fund."

"Now you're talking like a smart investor," Liz said.

"As difficult as it is not to panic, it is the worst thing you can do. Buying when the market is down is the smartest way to invest and investors who hold their securities during turbulent times will be rewarded. Just when you decide to sell and take your losses, the market will turn, and when it turns you won't be there to take advantage of the upswing. Don't forget that your investments to date are in your RRSP and you get a tax refund, which you should calculate into your overall return."

"Speaking of tax refunds, I received mine last week. Did anyone else get theirs?" Judy asked.

"Yes, we all have our refunds. It's great," Cathy said. "I would like to make a suggestion. Since we have accomplished so much this winter and we all have our investment plans in place and have received tax refunds, why don't we all chip in and have the barbeque catered."

"Brilliant! I agree," Annie said. "But let's hire some neigh-bourhood kids to clean up as well."

"Great idea, Annie," Cathy said. "We deserve it."

"I think that you are well on your way to understanding the markets. We have concentrated on learning for so long that I think we can revert back to our social meetings after today," Liz suggested.

"You mean that you are through guiding us, Liz?" Judy asked.

"I believe that you have the basic information needed to work very successfully with your financial advisor and continue on with your learning on a day-to-day basis," Liz explained.

"I agree. I know that I am able to follow the market and understand the meaning of the day's events. We are certainly much further ahead today than we were six months ago," Ruth commented.

"If you have a question I am still here, but I feel that you can find your way around the markets. Let's clean up some unfinished business today," Liz said. "One of the areas that we didn't get a chance to look at was your mutual fund purchase confirmations. Let's spend a few minutes now and see how you are doing."

"We all bought from different investment managers and the confirmation slips are all different and confusing, Liz," Judy said.

"Yes, if you buy directly from the manager, the confirmation comes directly from them and each one has a different reporting format. If a broker buys on your behalf, you'll probably receive a confirmation from the brokerage house as well as one from the management company. Because Annie, Judy and Cathy purchased only mutual funds, they went directly through to the manager, while Ruth's plan is at the brokerage firm and Barb's is at a trust company. Ruth and Barb really did not have a choice, as the only way they can buy stock in their RRSP is through a self-directed plan, which the mutual fund companies don't offer. Once the smaller plans have grown, the rest of you should transfer them to self-directed plans," Liz reminded them.

"I wasn't aware that you bought stock, Barb," Ruth stated.

"I didn't, I bought a closed-end mutual fund, one that invests in real estate and because it trades on the exchange, it can only be held in a self-directed RRSP," I explained.

"Remember, because you have elected to pay your annual trustee fee outside your plan, it is treated as an investment expense, as is a safety deposit box fee or interest paid on money borrowed to buy an investment," Liz reminded us.

"You mentioned interest expense when borrowing. Can you explain how that works?"

"Yes. Some investors borrow money to invest, just as Annie did with her RRSP contribution. This approach can be very risky if the investments acquired are securities and mutual funds and the market falls."

"Why, if you wait it out, the market will come back," Annie stated.

"That is true, but the lender may not be prepared to wait out a market correction. One of the major influences on the market in the correction of 1987 was lenders calling loans. They'll lend say 50 to 75 percent of the value of an investment on the day the investment is purchased. They will then monitor the price and if the value falls to below 75 percent of the price paid, the lender will phone and ask you for more money or securities to bring it back in line. At that point, the borrower must raise money to satisfy the lender. A lot of borrowing investors in 1987 had to sell other investments in order to raise cash, which further accelerated the fall in the market."

"Wow, that would have forced them to sell at the wrong time," Cathy said.

"Exactly, and that is the risk when borrowing to invest."

"So why do people borrow to invest?" Annie asked, puzzled.

"In a rising market a lot of money can be made by borrowing. If someone borrowed, say, $50,000 and invested that money in a stock or fund that doubled, they would sell, pay back the lender and have a $50,000 profit. The cost or interest charged by the lender could be deducted from income, except RRSP loan interest, which is not deductible."

"I guess it's true that it takes money to make money," Ruth said.

"Yes, but for average investors like us, I don't think borrowing is the answer, unless it is for your RRSP contribution. It is simply too risky."

"But what if we borrowed and paid the loan back, say, within a year?" Cathy asked.

"That can be a good strategy if you mean a forced savings plan. Nothing wrong with that approach, provided that at the end of a specific time frame, you own the investment outright. I think it is a good concept, and for some people, may be the only way to build an investment plan," Liz stated. "You can use the equity in your home as collateral and borrow, repay the loan over a period of five years and in some cases longer, and have an investment, free and clear. The interest on the loan would be tax deductible provided you can show a clear paper trail that the money was used for investment purposes."

"That's an interesting idea," Annie said, "Someone who strives to pay off their mortgage could use this strategy, say five or ten years before they retire. I wish I had known all of this years ago, before my dad retired. My mother's life would be so different today."

"Liz, would you please show me how to value my investments as of today. I find this confirmation is confusing," Judy asked, handing Liz the form.

"The information outlines what fund you purchased, the day you purchased it, which is called the trade date, and your account number. It indicates that you initiated a purchase - if you had sold instead, this would read redemption. It shows you the gross amount and then a sales charge and the percentage, or the word deferred. Yours shows deferred because your representative was paid by the fund manager, so there is no sales charge up front. Remember I said that if you redeem within a specified period you pay commission on a declining scale. The amount actually invested would be less if you had been charged an up-front fee. The price indicates the amount per share or unit that you paid and also how many shares you purchased. Most mutual funds are priced daily at the close of business and purchases or redemptions for that day are made at that price."

"You mean you won't know the price you are paying until the next day, unlike a stock which you could know the same day?" Ruth asked.

"That's right. The same situation applies when you sell. If you redeem, you receive the price at the close of business on the day the fund receives your request, and you learn the price that you received the next day," Liz explained. "If you multiply the number of shares by the purchase price, you'll come back to your original gross amount."

"Why are there three digits after the shares. It shows 232.558. Why not just round to 233?" Judy asked.

"Because you bought a specific dollar amount, the shares are extended to fractional shares. The mutual fund industry always takes the shares to at least three digits and some take it to four. They only round pennies, not shares. You paid $6.02 and bought 232.558 shares which equals $ 1,399.999 which is as close to the $1,400 you gave them as they can get."

"The $6.02 is referred to as my unit or per-share cost," Annie stated.

"Yes, and you should record your cost amount and keep it in a safe place, so that in the future you can calculate your gain or loss," Liz cautioned.

"I thought there was no tax within the RRSP, so why do you need to keep track of your cost?" Cathy asked.

"You are right about the tax, but don't forget your foreign content calculation. And someday you'll want to know what your return is and the only way to do that is to keep track yourself," Liz stated.

"That's the truth. Bob dealt with a company that left Canada five years ago and he had stock which he sold last year. He doesn't remember how much he paid for it, and he has no way of checking."

"That's right, most firms keep track for their clients, but they may not always be around, so you should set up a file and record every transaction."

"Let me understand, Liz. If I multiply the number of shares that I bought by the latest price in the newspaper, that will tell me what my investment is worth today?" Annie asked.

"Yes, please get the paper and tell me what it closed at yesterday. Look under the manager's name for your particular fund. Do you see it?" Liz asked.

"It says $6.24," Annie read.

"Hand me the calculator. Okay let's multiply $6.24 by the number of shares that you bought, 232.558. That gives you $1,451.16. You have made $ 51.16 in two months."

"Oh, I understand."

"Now let's see what that works out to on a percentage basis. If you divide your initial investment into the gain, that is $1,400 into $51.16, you'll get .0365 percent which is equal to a little better that 3.5 percent," Liz said calculating the figures.

"That's not very much."

"That is only for two months. Divide two into 3.5 percent gives you 1.75 percent per month. There are 12 months in a year, so multiply times 12 to get an approximate annualized return. Twelve times 1.75 percent equals 21 percent. If your investment continues to grow at a rate of 1.75 percent, every month for the balance of the year, you'll earn approximately $294.00 on your $1,400 initial investment or approximately 21 percent."

"Now I understand. That sure beats the bank," Annie said, pleased.

"Yes, but it won't do that every month. Some months it will be higher and some months lower," Liz cautioned.

"I brought one of Bob's confirmations on a fund he bought in January and it keeps going lower, Liz. Will you look at it, please," Ruth said. "This shows that he bought a mortgage fund and paid $9.97 per share. The price in the paper this morning is $9.92 so he is losing money."

"Not necessarily. A mortgage or a bond fund generally pays a dividend at the end of each month. The price at the close of each day represents the growth of the investment plus any income earned and not distributed, less the manager's expenses. When the income or dividends are paid, because the income amount was previously included in the daily price, the share price drops, but the shareholder receives a dividend in the form of shares. Although the price appears to be lower, the fund has issued more shares to him. If Bob telephones his broker tomorrow, he'll tell him how many shares he currently has. You are looking at an up-to-date price, but an historical share number status. Mutual fund managers generally provide semi-annual statements and then you'll be able to see the additional dividend purchases."

"That's great. I'll do that," Ruth said.

"Do all the funds pay dividends and does the price fall on all of them?" Cathy asked.

"Most funds pay a dividend if they have earned money either through dividends, interest income or capital gains received on the investments within the fund.

"Equity funds generally distribute the income at the end of the year, most of them on December 31, but as in Bob's case, mortgage funds, as well as most bond funds, pay monthly. You can elect to receive the income or, as in Bob's case, reinvest the dividend and buy more shares, which creates the compounding effect. And yes, the price will fall when the dividend is paid and that is the best time to buy them. People can create a tax problem for themselves if they buy a fund at the wrong time of the year."

"What do you mean?" Cathy asked.

"Let's take Judy's withdrawal plan. She bought it in March at a price of $10.46. It paid a handsome dividend the previous December. If it continues to grow throughout the year and in November it is, let's say, $12, anyone buying it then will be buying part of a dividend due to be paid in December, which instantly turns part of their capital into income, subject to tax for that year."

"So taxes really play a part in all of your investment planning," Ruth stated.

"No question, an investor shouldn't let tax considerations drive investments, but you should be aware of the ramifications of taxes. The RRSP is unaffected, but what is referred to as open or unregistered money has to be watched," Liz explained.

"What are all these letters in front of the fund name?" Anne said, peering up over the top of the paper.

"Remember that I explained that the paper uses a symbol to explain the different features attached to the funds?" Liz reminded us. "Newspapers are a fountain of information, even for stocks. They provide a legend so that you can sort through the information. For example Annie, the letter R means the fund is eligible for RRSPs."

"Oh, I see what you are saying, in this newspaper U means it is U.S. dollars, and X means it has paid a dividend. This is great," she said.

"And once a week or a month I find that the different newspapers provide an historical look at mutual funds," Ruth explained.

"What do you mean, Ruth?" Cathy asked.

"They break the funds into different categories, Canadian and International and by type of fund, and they show and rate their returns for one month, three months, one, two, three, five and 10 year periods. It is very helpful," Ruth commented.

"Yes, and I would suggest that you find out which newspaper runs these reports and when, and that you sit down once a month and review your investments. You can check every day, but you won't get an historical picture as you do in the monthly report," Liz suggested. "Also, you may find it confusing unless you look at the one-month and three-month history, because your fund may be down, but for the year, the fund history may show that it is up."

"Why is that?" Annie asked.

"Because you probably did not buy the same day as the paper is reporting. The one-year history is taken from the previous month-end price and compared to last year's same month and the months move every time they report."

"I see, I may not be looking at the exact same time frame," Annie said.

"That's right. It is important to check the one-and three-month number. The best way to verify your return is to subtract your current price from your cost, but make sure that you have the accurate number of shares. You may find, as we did with Bob's investment, that the price is down, but a dividend has been declared and you own more shares," Liz suggested.

"We've experienced a very volatile market over the past month. Can you list, in order, from the safest to the most volatile investments for us, Liz?" Cathy asked.

"Yes, certainly. The safest investment from a capital protection aspect would be Canada Savings Bonds and a GIC, when you haven't exceeded the CDIC insurance limit, then money market funds and Treasury Bills. I would lump all of these investments in one category and tell you that these are the safest investments if your first and foremost goal is the preservation of capital. Bonds, mortgages and bond and mortgage funds as well as strip coupons would be next on our scale of secure investments, but their values do fluctuate, depending on their quality, term to maturity and interest rates.

"Preferred shares or preferred share mutual funds would be classified next, depending on their quality and interest rates. Remember that interest rate changes will move the price up and down. I would then place balanced funds and asset allocation funds next, and in that order, because of their mixed portfolios. Canadian equity funds would be less volatile than international ones, because of currency exposure. U.S. funds would be less volatile than emerging market international funds and large-and medium-cap funds should be less volatile than small-cap funds."

"What about speciality funds, like gold or real estate? Where do they sit on the scale?" Annie asked.

"Investments that concentrate on one segment of the market are riskier than ones that are broadly diversified over many different industries. They would experience wider swings in their market price. In addition to the volatility, liquidity could be a problem," Liz explained.

"Even a gold mutual fund?" Annie asked.

"Yes, it could experience a liquidity problem if the manager is operating a small fund and investing in small mining companies with shares that are thinly traded."

"What do you mean thinly traded?" Ruth asked.

"Some company shares are held by a few large shareholders and when this happens, there may not be enough shares traded on a daily basis to create a demand for the stock, resulting in illiquidity," Liz said. "You may also want to ask your financial advisor for the volatility rating on mutual funds, as they are rated based on the historic value. Generally the higher the number the greater the volatility."

"That's a good idea, I'm going to check mine with Doug," Annie said.

"Yes, and you'll find that the speciality fund that you are buying on a monthly basis will be rated as more volatile than your other investment," Liz predicted.

"Liz, I read about a fund that gives you an additional tax break because they are investing in start-up companies. Can you explain, please, what they are referring to?" Annie asked.

"Yes, that is called a labour-sponsored investment, which provides, under certain provincial regulations, additional tax credits for investing in the fund. They in turn invest in small-and medium-sized businesses wanting to expand or restructure. This kind of investing inherently carries an additional risk but offers the potential for a good return. There are only a few of these types of funds in Canada and there is a five-year holding period, during which time, with few exceptions, you must repay the tax credits originally received if you redeem. The tax credit is over and above the deduction that you get through your RRSP."

"That sounds like a good concept," Annie said.

"Yes, it does. These funds are new but for a long-term investment, it is a good concept. Remember that they are typically investing in private companies and private corporations are sometimes difficult to value and sell. The manager has restrictions and is required to maintain a minimum of 20 percent of the fund's assets in high-quality government securities to satisfy redemption requests. They monitor the fund constantly in order to prevent a liquidity problem if ever a situation occurs where more people want to redeem than they have cash to satisfy."

"That's a great deal. I think I'll ask my advisor about this fund next RRSP season," Judy said.

"There are so many things to remember!"Ruth exclaimed, "I suspect that by not realizing all the different investment options and strategies that the different funds employ, a person could very easily put their whole life savings at risk unless they work with a knowledgeable financial advisor."

"That's right, Ruth, but risk is everywhere, and in addition to that, because we can't predict the future, we can't be sure that what we are doing is right. But I do know that it is risky to sit idle and not take advantage of opportunities. Every wealthy individual in the world, unless they have inherited their money or won a lottery, has earned it by taking a risk," Liz said. "Our goal from the beginning has been to build our net worth in order to secure our future. Having a long-term perspective and through investing in the equity market there is no question in my mind that we'll succeed."

"I guess 'slow and steady wins the race' would be the best investment strategy," Ruth quoted.

"That's so right, Ruth. To finish up, why don't we just summarize what we have learned - not all of it, but the key points to remember, such as, when interest rate rise bond prices fall."

"Not only bonds but bond mutual funds, mortgage funds, preferred shares and preferred mutual funds," Cathy added.

"The longer you have until retirement, the less money you need to invest monthly," Annie said.

"Good one, Annie! And the closer you are to retirement, the more conservative your investments should be," Judy stated. "I think this is the one that Ruth has not yet grasped."

"I'm going to ignore that remark. Investing in foreign funds adds an element of risk due to currency fluctuation," Ruth responded.

"Take advantage of a drop in prices, buy low and sell high, or better still buy on a monthly basis," I said.

"You would think of that, Barb," Liz said. "What about diversification?"

"Diversification reduces your risk," Annie offered.

"Remain in liquid investments in order to take advantage of good opportunities," Judy said.

"Most of all be a long-term investor," Ruth concluded.

"By Jove, I think you've got it. Good luck everyone."

Addresses & Phone Numbers

Canadian Shareowners Association
1090 University Avenue West
P.O.Box 7337,
Windsor, Ontario N9C 4E9
1-519-252-1555
Fax 1-519-252-9570

The Canadian Securities Institute
121 King St. W., Suite 1550
P.O. Box 113
Toronto, Ontario M5H 3T9
1-416-364-9130
Fax 1-416-359-0486

The Toronto Stock Exchange
The Exchange Tower
2 First Canadian Place
P.O. Box 450
Toronto, Ontario M5X 1J2
1-416-947-4700
Fax 1-416-947-4662

The Vancouver Stock Exchange
609 Granville St.
P.O. Box 10333
Vancouver, B.C. V7Y 1H1
1-604-689-3334
Fax 1-604-688-5041

The Montreal Exchange
800 Victoria Square
Montreal, Quebec H4Z 1A9
1-514-871-2424
Fax 1-514-871-3533

The Alberta Stock Exchange
300 Fifth Avenue S.W., 3rd Flr.
Calgary, Alberta T2P 3C4
1-403-974-7400
Fax 1-403-237-0450

The Investment Funds Institute
151 Yonge Street, 5th Flr.
Toronto, Ontario M5C 2W7
1-416-861-9937

**Canadian Institute
of Financial Planning**
151 Yonge St., Suite 503
Toronto, Ontario M5C 2W7
1-416-865-1237
Fax 1-416-366-1527

FinancialXPress
The First Financial Magazine for Women by Women
914 Carlaw Avenue
Toronto, Ontario M4K 3L3

ORDER A GIFT FOR
A FRIEND, MOTHER, SISTER,
DAUGHTER & EVEN YOUR HUSBAND OR SON

BECAUSE THEY ARE WORTH IT TOO!

Please forward _____ copies of "You're Worth It" to me at:

NAME _____

ADDRESS _____

_____

_____ POSTAL CODE _____

No of Copies _____ x $ 16.95 = $ _____

Postage and Handling $ ___3.00___

G.S.T @ 7% (Canadian Residents Only) $ _____

I have enclosed a cheque in the amount of $ _____

TOTAL

TO: Raintree Communications
      c/o 755 The Queensway East, Suite 105
      Mississauga, Ontario L4Y 4C5

Bulk orders contact directly by
Fax 1-905-897-2011